D1443929

SRA ART Connections

Level 6

Authors

Rosalind Ragans, Ph.D., Senior Author

Willis "Bing" Davis   Jane Rhoades Hudak, Ph.D.   Bunyan Morris
Tina Farrell   Gloria McCoy   Nan Yoshida

Contributing Author

Jackie Ellett

Education Division
The Music Center of Los Angeles County

Columbus, OH

The **McGraw-Hill** Companies

Authors

Senior Author
Dr. Rosalind Ragans, Ph.D.
Associate Professor Emerita
Georgia Southern University

Willis "Bing" Davis
Associate Professor Emeritus
Central State University - Ohio
President & Founder of
SHANGO: The Center for the
Study of African American
Art & Culture

Tina Farrell
Assistant Superintendent
Curriculum and Instruction
Clear Creek Independent
School District,
League City, Texas

Jane Rhoades Hudak, Ph.D.
Professor of Art
Georgia Southern University

Gloria McCoy
Former President
Texas Art Education Association
Spring Branch Independent
School District, Texas

Bunyan Morris
Art Teacher
Effingham County School
System, Springfield, Georgia

Nan Yoshida
Art Education Consultant
Retired Art Supervisor
Los Angeles Unified School
District
Los Angeles, California

SRAonline.com

Send all inquiries to:
SRA/McGraw-Hill
8787 Orion Place
Columbus, OH 43240-4027

Printed in the United States of America.

ISBN 0-07-601825-3

4 5 6 7 8 9 RRW 10 09 08 07 06

The McGraw-Hill Companies

Contributors

Contributing Author
Jackie Ellett, Ed. S.
Elementary Art Teacher
Duncan Creek Elementary School
Hoschton, Georgia

Contributing Writer
Lynda Kerr, NBCT
Ed.D. Candidate, Art Teacher
Henry County, Georgia

Artsource® Music, Dance, Theatre Lessons
Mark Slavkin, Vice President
for Education, The Music Center of
Los Angeles County
Michael Solomon, Managing Director
Music Center Education Division
Melinda Williams, Concept Originator and
Project Director
Susan Cambigue-Tracey, Project Coordinator
and Writer
Madeleine Dahm, Movement and Dance
Connection Writer
Keith Wyffels, Staff Assistance
Maureen Erbe, Logo Design

More about Aesthetics
Richard W. Burrows
Executive Director, Institute for Arts
Education
San Diego, California

Safe Use of Art Materials
Mary Ann Boykin
Director, The Art School for Children and
Young Adults
University of Houston–Clear Lake
Houston, Texas

Museum Education
Marilyn J. S. Goodman
Director of Education
Solomon R. Guggenheim Museum
New York, New York

Resources for Students with Disabilities
Mandy Yeager
Ph.D. Candidate
The University of North Texas
Denton, Texas

Music Connections
Kathy Mitchell
Music Teacher
Eagan, Minnesota

Student Activities

Cassie Appleby
Glen Oaks Elementary School
McKinney, Texas

Maureen Banks
Kester Magnet School
Van Nuys, California

Christina Barnes
Webb Bridge Middle School
Alpharetta, Georgia

Beth Benning
Willis Jepson Middle School
Vacaville, California

Chad Buice
Craig Elementary School
Snellville, Georgia

Beverly Broughton
Gwinn Oaks Elementary School
Snellville, Georgia

Missy Burgess
Jefferson Elementary School
Jefferson, Georgia

Marcy Cincotta-Smith
Benefield Elementary School
Lawrenceville, Georgia

Joanne Cox
Kittredge Magnet School
Atlanta, Georgia

Carolyn Y. Craine
McCracken County Schools
Paducah, Kentucky

Jackie Ellett
Duncan Creek Elementary School
Hoschton, Georgia

Tracie Flynn
Home School
Rushville, Indiana

Phyllis Glenn
Malcom Bridge Elementary
Bogart, Georgia

Dallas Gillespie
Dacula Middle School
Dacula, Georgia

Dr. Donald Gruber
Clinton Junior High School
Clinton, Illinois

Karen Heid
Rock Springs Elementary School
Lawrenceville, Georgia

Alisa Hyde
Southwest Elementary
Savannah, Georgia

Kie Johnson
Oconee Primary School
Watkinsville, Georgia

Sallie Keith, NBCT
West Side Magnet School
LaGrange, Georgia

Letha Kelly
Grayson Elementary School
Grayson, Georgia

Diana Kimura
Amestoy Elementary School
Gardena, California

Desiree LaOrange
Barkley Elementary School
Fort Campbell, Kentucky

Deborah Lackey-Wilson
Roswell North Elementary
Roswell, Georgia

Dawn Laird
Goforth Elementary School
Clear Creek, Texas

Mary Lazzari
Timothy Road Elementary School
Athens, Georgia

Michelle Leonard
Webb Bridge Middle School
Alpharetta, Georgia

Lynn Ludlam
Spring Branch ISD
Houston, Texas

Mark Mitchell
Fort Daniel Elementary School
Dacula, Georgia

Martha Moore
Freeman's Mill Elementary School
Dacula, Georgia

Connie Niedenthal
Rushville Elementary
Rushville, Indiana

Barbara Patisaul
Oconee County Elementary
School
Watkinsville, Georgia

Elizabeth Paulos-Krasle
Social Circle Elementary
Social Circle, Georgia

Jane Pinneau
Rocky Branch Elementary School
Watkinsville, Georgia

Marilyn Polin
Cutler Ridge Middle School
Miami, Florida

Michael Ramsey
Graves County Schools
Mayfield, Kentucky

Rosemarie Sells
Social Circle Elementary
Social Circle, Georgia

Jean Neelen–Siegel
Baldwin School
Alhambra, California

Debra Smith
McIntosh County School System
Darien, Georgia

Patricia Spencer
Harmony Elementary School
Buford, Georgia

Melanie Stokes
Smiley Elementary School
Ludowici, Georgia

Rosanne Stutts
Davidson Fine Arts School
Augusta, Georgia

Fran Sullivan
South Jackson Elementary School
Athens, Georgia

Kathy Valentine
Home School
Burkburnett, Texas

Debi West
Rock Springs Elementary School
Lawrenceville, Georgia

Sherry White
Bauerschlag Elementary School
League City, Texas

Patricia Wiesen
Cutler Ridge Middle School
Miami, Florida

Deayna Woodruff
Loveland Middle School
Loveland, Ohio

Gil Young
El Rodeo School
Beverly Hills, California

Larry A. Young
Dacula Elementary School
Dacula, Georgia

Table of Contents

◀ **Gustav Klimt.**
Fulfillment.

Unit 1 Line, Shape, Form, and Space

▲ **Auguste Renior.**
Young Spanish Woman with a Guitar.

Unit 2 Color and Texture

▲ **Max Weber.**
Chinese Restaurant.

Unit 3 Rhythm, Movement, and Pattern

Unit 4 Balance and Emphasis

◀ **Paul Gauguin.**
The Brooding Woman.

Unit 6 Variety, Harmony, and Unity

Technique Tips

Activity Tips

What Is Art?

Art is . . .

Painting is color applied to a flat surface.

▲ **Vincent Van Gogh.** (French). *Houses at Auvers.* 1890.

Oil on canvas. $29\frac{3}{4} \times 24\frac{3}{8}$ inches (75.56×61.93 cm.). Museum of Fine Arts, Boston, Massachusetts.

Drawing is the process of making art with lines.

▲ **Pablo Picasso.** (Spanish). *Portrait of Dora Maar.* 1938.

Pencil on paper mounted on fiberboard. $30\frac{9}{16} \times 22\frac{7}{16}$ inches (77.62×57 cm.). Hirshhorn Museum and Sculpture Garden, Smithsonian Institution, Washington, D.C.

Sculpture is art that fills up space.

▲ **David Bates.** (American). *Seated Man #4.* 1995.

Painted wood. $88 \times 37\frac{1}{2} \times 45\frac{1}{2}$ inches ($223.52 \times 95.25 \times 115.57$ cm.). Dallas Museum of Art, Dallas, Texas.

Architecture is the art of designing and constructing buildings.

▲ **Jørn Oberg Utzon.** (Danish). *Opera House.* 1957–1973.

Sydney, Australia.

Printmaking is the process of transferring an original image from one prepared surface to another.

▲ **Katsushika Hokusai.** (Japanese.) *Winter Loneliness,* from *One Hundred Poems Explained by the Nurse.* 1839.

Woodcut. $10\frac{1}{16} \times 14\frac{1}{2}$ inches (25.5 × 36.8 cm.). Honolulu Academy of Art, Honolulu, Hawaii

Ceramics is the art of making objects with clay.

▲ **Artist Unknown.** (Kongo peoples, Congo and Democratic Republic of Congo.) **Bowl.** Late-nineteenth to early-twentieth century.

Ceramic and resin. $5\frac{7}{8} \times 4\frac{1}{8} \times 5\frac{7}{8}$ inches (14.9 × 10.49 × 14.94 cm.). National Museum of African Art, Smithsonian Institution, Washington, D.C.

Photography is the act of capturing an image on film.

◀ **Eliot Elisofon.** (American). *Asante Paramount Chief Nana Akyanfuo Akowuah Dateh II, Akwamuhene of Kumase.* 1970.

Photograph. National Museum of African Art, Smithsonian Institution, Washington, D.C.

A mask is a covering for the face to be used in ceremonies and other events.

▲ **Charlie James.** (Southern Kwakiutl.) *Sun Tranformation Mask.* Early nineteenth century.

Royal British Columbia Museum, British Columbia, Canada.

Art is created by people

► to communicate ideas.

► to express feelings.

► to give us well-designed objects.

What Is Art?

Every work of art has three parts.

Subject

The objects you can recognize are the subject matter of a work of art. When a work has no recognizable objects, the elements of art such as lines, shapes, colors, and so on become the subject of the work.

Composition

The composition of the work is the way the artist has used the principles to organize the elements of art.

Content

The content is the message the artwork communicates. Content is the meaning of the work. If the work is functional, such as a chair or clothing, then the content is the function of the object.

▶ In which work of art do you think the subject matter is very important?

▶ In which artwork do you think composition is most important?

▶ Which work seems to have the strongest message? Explain.

▶ Which artwork's meaning relates to its function?

Benny Andrews. (American). *Grandmother's Dinner.* 1992.

Oil on canvas. 72 × 52 inches (182.88 × 132.08 cm.). Ogden Museum of Southern Art, New Orleans, Louisiana.

▲ **William Sharp.** (English/American). *Great Water Lily of America.* 1854.

Chromolithograph on woven white paper. $21\frac{1}{4}$ × 27 inches (53.98 × 68.58 cm.). Amon Carter Museum, Fort Worth, Texas.

▲ **Artist Unknown.** (Maya/Huipil). *Huipil Weaving.* c. 1950.

Backstrap woven plain weave with supplementary-weft pattern, silk on cotton. 50 × $14\frac{1}{2}$ inches (127 × 36.83 cm.). Museum of International Folk Art, Santa Fe, New Mexico.

▲ **Mosche Safdie.** (Israeli). *Habitat.* 1967.

Concrete. Montreal, Canada.

What Is Art?

Subject Matter

Artists make art about many subjects. *Subject matter* is the content of an artist's work. For example, the subject of a painting can be a vase of flowers or a self-portrait. This subject matter is easy to see. The subject matter is harder to understand when the artwork stands for something beyond itself. Look at the artwork on these pages. Notice the different kinds of subject matter.

Still Life

▲ **Paul Cézanne.** (French). *Still Life with Basket of Apples.* 1895.

Oil on canvas. $23\frac{3}{5} \times 31\frac{1}{2}$ inches (60 × 80 cm.). The Art Institute of Chicago, Chicago, Illinois.

Landscape

▲ **Z. Vanessa Helder.** (American). *Rocks and Concrete.* c. 1940.

Watercolor on paper. 19 × 15$\frac{7}{8}$ inches (48.26 × 40.34 cm.). Cheney Cowles Museum, Spokane, Washington.

What Is Art?

Genre

▲ **Winslow Homer.** (American.) *Nooning.* c. 1872.

Oil on canvas. $13\frac{5}{16} \times 19\frac{5}{8}$ inches (33.02 × 48.26 cm.). Wadsworth Atheneum, Hartford, Connecticut.

Nonobjective

◀ **Natalya Goncharova.** (Russian). *Maquillage.* 1913.
Gouache on paper. $4\frac{3}{8} \times 6\frac{3}{8}$ inches (11.13 × 16.21 cm.). Dallas Museum of Art, Dallas, Texas.

Portrait

◀ **Elizabeth Catlett.** (American). *Sharecropper.* 1970.
Color linocut. 26 × 22 inches (66.04 × 55.88 cm.). Smithsonian American Art Museum, Washington, D.C.

What Is Art?

Allegory

▲ **Jan van Eyck.** (Flemish.) *Portrait of Giovanni Arnolfini and His wife Giovanna Cenami.* 1434.

Oil on wood panel. 32 x 23 inches. The National Gallery, London, England.

Symbolism

▲ **Artist Unknown.** (Huichol People/Mexico). *Mother of the Eagles.* 1991.

Braided yarn embedded in vegetable wax on wood. $15\frac{3}{4} \times 19\frac{1}{2}$ inches (40 × 49.53 cm.). Private collection.

Elements of Art

Art is a language. The words of the language are the elements of art.

Line

Shape

Form

Space

Color

Value

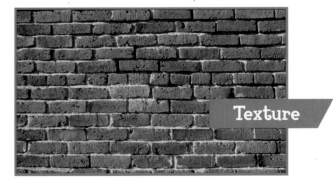
Texture

Principles of Art

Artists organize their artwork using the principles of art.

Pattern

Rhythm

Balance

Emphasis

Harmony

Variety

Unity

▲ **Frida Kahlo.** (Mexican). *Frida y Diego Rivera.* 1931.
....
Oil on canvas. 39⅜ × 31 inches (100.01 × 78.74 cm.). San Francisco Museum of Modern Art, San Francisco, California.

Art History and Culture

Look at the artwork.

▶ What people or objects do you see?

▶ Do they look like people and objects you see around you today? Explain.

Look at the caption.

▶ When was the artwork created?

▶ What can you learn about the artist?

Learn more.

▶ Do some research to find out more about the artist, the artwork, and the time period.

▲ **Frida Kahlo.** (Mexican). *Frida y Diego Rivera.* 1931.

Oil on canvas. $39\frac{3}{8} \times 31$ inches (100.01 × 78.74 cm.). San Francisco Museum of Modern Art, San Francisco, California.

Look

▶ Look at the work of art. What sounds, smells, or feelings are in this work of art?

▶ What happened just before and just after in this work of art?

▶ What kind of music would be playing in this work of art?

Look Inside

▶ Imagine you are one of these people. Who are you? What are you thinking? How do you feel?

▶ If you could add yourself to the painting, what would you look like? What would you be doing?

▶ Act out or tell the story in this work of art with a beginning, a middle, and an end.

▶ Draw what you can't see in this work of art. Are there hidden images that should be revealed?

Look Outside

▶ How is this like or different from your own world?

▶ What does the artist want you to know or think about in this work of art?

▶ Describe your journey in viewing this work of art. Include your thoughts, ideas, and changes in thinking.

▶ What will you remember about this work?

About Art

▲ **Frida Kahlo.** (Mexican). *Frida y Diego Rivera*. 1931.

Oil on canvas. 39$\frac{3}{8}$ × 31 inches (100.01 × 78.74 cm.). San Francisco Museum of Modern Art, San Francisco, California.

Art Criticism

Describe

► List everything you see in this painting. Be sure to describe the people and their clothing.

Analyze

► How has the artist used line, shape, color, value, space, and texture?

► What kind of balance has the artist used?

► Has the artist used emphasis to make us notice one thing more than others?

Interpret

► What is happening?

► What is the artist telling us about these two people?

Decide

► Have you ever seen another artwork like this?

► Is it successful because it is realistic?

► Is it successful because it is well-organized?

► Is it successful because you have strong feelings when you study it?

▲ **Frida Kahlo.** (Mexican). *Frida y Diego Rivera.* 1931.
Oil on canvas. 39⅜ × 31 inches (100.01 × 78.74 cm.). San Francisco Museum of Modern Art, San Francisco, California.

How does an artist create a work of art?

Art is a process. You can follow the same steps to create your own work of art.

1. Get an idea.

▶ Artists get inspiration from many places. Look around you. People, objects, and scenes may provide inspiration for a work of art.

2. Plan your work.

▶ Do you want your artwork to be two-dimensional or three-dimensional?

▶ Decide what media you want to use.

▶ What materials will you need?

3. Make a sketch.

▶ Think about how you want your artwork to look. Sketch several ideas.

▶ If your artwork will be three-dimensional, sketch it from different points of view.

▶ Then choose the best idea.

4. Use the media.

▶ Make an artwork based on your best idea. You may want to practice using the materials first.

▶ When making your composition, remember the elements and principles of art. How can you use them to make your artwork say what you want it to say?

5. Share your final work.

▶ Evaluate your work using the four steps of art criticism. What do you like best about your work? What would you do differently next time?

Safety

▶ Use art materials only on your artwork.

▶ Keep art materials out of your mouth, eyes and ears.

▶ Use scissors and other sharp tools carefully. Keep your fingers away from the cutting blades.

▶ Wash your hands after using the art materials.

▶ Wear an art shirt or smock to protect your clothes.

▶ Use only art materials with a "nontoxic" label.

- ▶ Return art materials to their proper storage place.
- ▶ Be careful not to breathe chalk or clay dust.
- ▶ Use only new and clean foam trays.
- ▶ Do not walk around the room with sharp tools in your hand.
- ▶ Be aware of others in your work space.
- ▶ Always follow your teacher's directions when using the art materials.

Line, Shape, Form, and Space

Artists use line, shape, form, and space to create a variety of works of art.

Gustav Klimt's use of line, shape, form, and space in *Fulfillment* makes it an eye-catching work of art. Each time a viewer looks at this piece, he or she will notice something new. Klimt is known for creating lively portraits and colorful landscapes.

◀ **Gustav Klimt.** (Austrian). *Die Erfüllung (Fulfillment).* 1905–1909.

Mixed media with gold leaf on paper. $76\frac{3}{8} \times 47\frac{5}{8}$ inches (194 × 121 cm.). Österreichisches Museum für angewandte Kunst, Vienna, Austria.

Artists use **lines** to create two-dimensional works of art.

▶ What types of lines do you see in the background?

Artists use **shapes** to represent objects found in nature and made by people.

▶ What types of shapes do you see on the clothes?

Forms are used by artists to create three-dimensional sculptures and architectural structures.

▶ Are there any forms in this work of art? Explain.

Artists use **space** to create two- and three-dimensional works of art.

▶ Do the people in the painting look like they are standing far from the wall? Explain.

In This Unit you will learn about different types of lines and shapes and how artists use them in different kinds of art. You will also learn about three-dimensional forms and about techniques used to create space. Here are the topics you will study:
▶ Line
▶ Shape
▶ Form
▶ Space
▶ Depth
▶ Perspective
▶ Positive and Negative Space

Gustav Klimt
(1862–1918)

Gustav Klimt was born near Vienna, Austria, and was part of an artistic family. His father was an engraver of gold and silver. One of his brothers was a goldsmith, and another brother was a painter. At the age of fourteen, Klimt enrolled in art school. He did not gain world-wide fame until the mid-twentieth century and was known only in the European art community up to that time. He preferred his art to speak for itself, rather than for him to talk about it.

Line and Qualities of Line

Look at *Plate 24* and *Ceremonial Skirt* on these pages. Matisse created the illustration of the swan for a book of poems titled *Poésies,* by Stéphane Mallarmé. Matisse incorporated the curved lines of the lettering into his illustration. He also used line to communicate the shape of the swan. *Ceremonial Skirt* is from Indonesia. The decorative design is applied to the top of the tapestry using **embroidery** techniques. The swan illustration and the figures in the cloth both include straight and curved lines. Notice that although the same types of lines are used in both works, they are used differently.

▲ **Henri Matisse.** (French). *Plate 24* from *Poésies* by Stéphane Mallarmé. 1932.

Etching. 13 × 9¾ inches (33.02 × 24.76 cm.). Museum of Modern Art, New York, New York.

 Art History and Culture

What years are included in the nineteenth and twentieth centuries?

Study both works of art to discover more about lines and how they can be used.

▶ What types of lines do you recognize? What type of line is used most often in both works?

▶ How are the lines in *Ceremonial Skirt* different from those in *Plate 24*? How are they the same?

▶ Describe the edges of the swan figure by Matisse.

▶ How were lines used to fill in the details of the swan figure?

◀ **Artist unknown.** (Flores/Indonesia). *Ceremonial Skirt.* Nineteenth century.

Cotton, glass beads, shell, and metal. $68\frac{1}{2} \times 31\frac{1}{4}$ inches (173.99 × 79.38 cm.). Dallas Museum of Art, Dallas, Texas.

Aesthetic Perception

Design Awareness Look around the classroom and notice the shapes of objects. What types of lines do you see most often?

Types of Lines

Artists use lines to lead the eyes through a work of art. A **line** is the path of a moving point through space. When looking at a line, a person's eyes will follow the path of its direction. Lines can look different. They can be thick or thin, short or long, and rough or smooth. A **contour line.** defines the edges and surface ridges of an object. Artists use various types of lines and line qualities when creating contour drawings.

Vertical lines move up and down and are inactive. They appear to be at rest and give the feeling of stability. Artists use vertical lines to show pride and stiffness in their work.

Horizontal lines move from side to side. They too are inactive and give the feeling of stability, calm, and quiet. They make us feel relaxed and content.

Diagonal lines move on a slant. They are active and express a feeling of instability. Artists use them to show excitement, instability, and activity. These lines often make us feel uncomfortable or tense.

Zigzag lines are made by joining diagonal lines. They are very active and express feelings of confusion and excitement.

Curved lines bend and change gradually or turn inward to form spirals. They express calm flowing activity. A spiral curves around, leading your eye toward a central point.

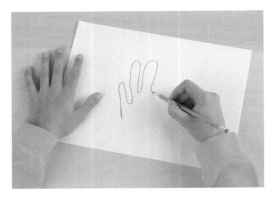

Practice

Use different types of lines to create blind contour drawings.

1. Look at your hand. Study its outline, or contours. Use a pencil, and draw a blind contour drawing of your hand.

2. Find an object in the room and create another blind contour drawing.

3. What type of lines did you use in each drawing? Describe how your eyes moved when you created your contours.

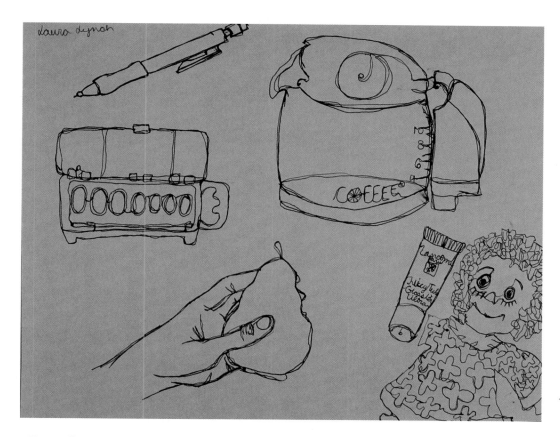

◀ **Laura Lynch.**
Age 12.

Think about what lines and line qualities this student artist used in the contour drawing.

Creative Expression

Find an object, or objects, and create a contour drawing using different types of lines.

1. Look over the directions you wrote in your Art Journal on how to make a contour drawing. Make a practice drawing of your object, or objects, following your directions.

2. Using a marker, make a second drawing of the same object.

3. Make some lines thick and some lines thin. You may pick up your marker and look at your paper to make the thick and thin lines. Always concentrate on the contours of your object.

4. Look at your first contour drawing and compare it to your second one.

Art Criticism

Describe What object did you select?

Analyze List the lines and line qualities you used in your contour drawings. What type of line did you use most often?

Interpret Give your completed work a title. What did you notice when you compared your first drawing with your second?

Decide Do you feel your contour drawing was a success? Explain.

Geometric and Free-Form Shapes

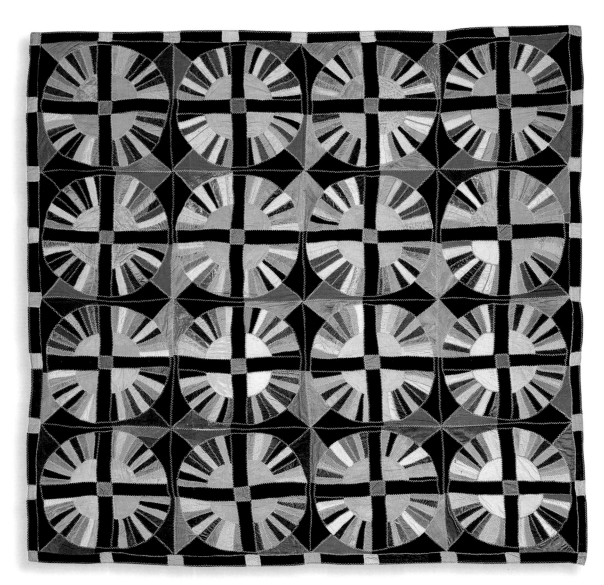

Look at both of the quilts on these pages. The design for *Quilt* is called a "fan." Each circle is made of four fans, or quilt squares, which are sewn together by hand. *Pictorial Quilt* is an **appliqué;** it was made with cloth cutouts made from fabric scraps. The shapes were arranged to tell a story.

▲ **Artist unknown.** (American). *Quilt.* c. 1885.

Pieced and embroidered silk, velvet, velveteen, and cotton sateen. $69\frac{1}{4} \times 68\frac{1}{4}$ inches (175.9 × 173.4 cm.). Museum of International Folk Art, Santa Fe, New Mexico.

 Art History and Culture

Why might a quilt be kept in a family for many years?

Study both quilts to become aware of how the artists used a variety of shapes.

▶ Can you find any rectangles, squares, circles, triangles, or diamonds in either quilt?

▶ Do you see any free-form shapes in the quilts?

▶ Do you recognize any objects in either of the quilts? Explain.

▶ What shapes are repeated in both quilts? How do you think the artists made these shapes?

▲ **Harriet Powers.**
(American). *Pictorial Quilt.* c. 1895–98.
. . . .
Cotton with cotton and metallic yarns. $68\frac{7}{8} \times 105$ inches (174.96 × 266.7 cm.). Museum of Fine Arts, Boston, Massachusetts.

Aesthetic Perception

Design Awareness Pick up your textbook and look at it from different angles. What shapes do you see? Now think of a leaf. How is the shape of the leaf different from that of the textbook?

Types of Shapes: Geometric and Free-Form

A **shape** is a two-dimensional area that is measured by height and width. Shapes can be solid, like a painted square, or outlined, like a drawing of a square. All shapes can be categorized as being either geometric or free-form.

Geometric shapes are exact and have mathematical measurements. Road signs, architecture, and many pieces of furniture are made of geometric shapes. There are three basic types of geometric shapes: circle, square, and triangle. By combining these shapes, artists can create **complex geometric shapes.** These combinations include an oval, rectangle, diamond, parallelogram, trapezoid, pentagon, hexagon, and octagon.

Trapezoid   Parallelogram   Pentagon   Hexagon   Octagon

Free-form shapes are irregular or uneven. Artists often use free-form shapes to represent things found in nature. Your shadow is an example of a free-form shape.

Practice

Design a pattern for a pictorial quilt square using geometric and free-form shapes.

1. Select one piece of colored construction paper as a background. Select contrasting pieces of paper to cut into a variety of shapes. Include at least one geometric and one free-form shape in the design. Try making complex geometric shapes.

2. Arrange your shapes on the background paper. Try overlapping smaller shapes onto larger shapes. Place your pattern pieces in a plastic sandwich bag to be used later.

◀ **Savannah Ankerich.**
Age 12.

Think about the types of shapes this student artist used in the pictorial quilt square.

Creative Expression

What scene from a story would you like to illustrate? Use both geometric and free-form shapes to design a pictorial quilt square.

1. Collect your pattern pieces from the Practice activity. Select a background square in the color that best depicts the time or place of your scene. Select various colors of felt for each of your pattern pieces.

2. Use a piece of chalk or a pencil to outline the paper shapes onto the felt pieces. Cut out the felt shapes and arrange them on the background square. Secure your shapes with either straight pins or a dot of craft glue.

3. Thread your needle and stitch the cut shapes into place on the background. Look at the embroidery Technique Tips on page 214 to get ideas for different stitches to use.

Art Criticism

Describe What scene did you select? Describe the scene you depicted.

Analyze Create two columns labeled *Geometric shapes* and *Free-form shapes*. List all of the objects in your quilt square under the appropriate shape. What type of shape did you use most often? Did you use any complex geometric shapes in your final design?

Interpret What mood or emotions are depicted in your square?

Decide Do you feel your quilt square successfully tells this part of the story? Explain.

Geometric Forms

Look at the two sculptures on these pages. *Cubi XVII* is made of several simple metal forms that have been welded together. David Smith intended for this sculpture to be viewed in an outdoor landscape. He finished the surface to reflect the natural light and the colors surrounding the sculpture. George Hart also used a simple form to create his sculpture. The surface design that makes up *Roads Untaken* is based on a mathematical formula. Hart created his form by combining four different types of wood.

◄ **David Smith.** (American).
Cubi XVII. 1963.
Polished stainless steel. $107\frac{3}{4} \times 64\frac{3}{8} \times 38\frac{1}{8}$ inches
($273.69 \times 163.53 \times 96.83$ cm.). Dallas Museum
of Art, Texas.

 Art History and Culture

Both *Cubi XVII* and *Roads Untaken* belong to the modern art period.

Study how the two artists used geometric forms in the works of art.

▶ What do the forms in each sculpture remind you of?

▶ Describe the shapes used in the design of *Roads Untaken*. Are any of these shapes used in *Cubi XVII*? Explain.

▶ How many surfaces do you think are in each of the square and rectangular forms in *Cubi XVII*? What about the form in *Roads Untaken*?

▲ **George Hart.** (American).
Roads Untaken. 1998.
. . . .
Exotic hardwoods with walnut grout. 17-inch
diameter (43.18 cm.). Private Collection.

Aesthetic Perception

Design Awareness Look around the classroom for an eraser, a small ball, a small box, and a pencil container. Place these objects on an overhead projector. Project their shadows onto a screen or wall. What shapes do you see?

Using Forms

Forms are three-dimensional objects that are measured by height, width, and depth. They have a thickness and can be viewed from more than two sides. Humans are forms. The chair you are sitting on and the building you are in are examples of forms. The type of forms used most often in objects made by people are called geometric forms.

Geometric forms, like geometric shapes, are based on mathematical formulas with precise measurements. For example the end of a cylinder is a circle, and a sphere is circular. Think about a square box. Because it is three-dimensional, it is called a cube. It is based on the geometric shape called a square. The three-dimensional form of a rectangle is called a rectangular solid. A cone or pyramid is the three-dimensional form of a triangle.

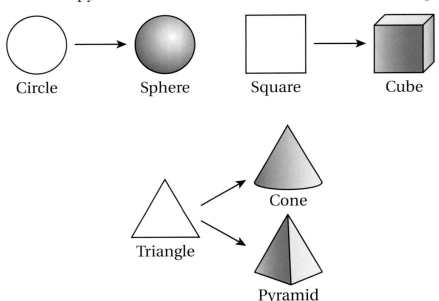

Circle   Sphere   Square   Cube

Triangle   Cone   Pyramid

Practice

Design a nonobjective sculpture based upon geometric forms.

1. Select either three or five geometric forms from the box of wood scraps. Look at them carefully from different directions and different angles.

2. Stack the forms in different arrangements. Look at the stacked sculpture from different angles.

3. How do the forms look from different angles? What would they look like if they were made from another material, such as steel?

◀ **Calvin Banks.**
Age 11.

Think about the geometric forms used by this student artist to construct the sculpture.

Creative Expression

Use three or five geometric forms to construct a nonobjective sculpture.

1. Look at the sketches in your Art Journal and collect the wooden forms you will need.

2. Use either wood glue or craft glue to put your sculpture together. You may need to use a hot-glue gun and sticks for those pieces that will not hold together. Ask your teacher for assistance with this.

3. As you glue your pieces together, see if your sculpture will stand on its own. You may need to make adjustments to your sculpture as you work.

4. Apply acrylic paint to your sculpture once the glue has dried completely. You may want to test colors on a scrap piece of paper before using it on the wood.

Art Criticism

Describe What materials did you use to create your sculpture? How many forms did you use?

Analyze What types of geometric forms did you use? Which form was used as your base? Why? What color or colors did you use to finish your sculpture?

Interpret Give your finished sculpture a title. Explain why you chose this title.

Decide Would you have liked to use another material for your sculpture? Where would you like to have it displayed? Why?

Free-Form Form

▲ **Paul A. Baliker.**
(American). *Fish Story.*

Bronze. Coles Garden, Northwest
Territory. Oklahoma City, Oklahoma.

Look at the sculptures on these pages. Artists often look to nature for inspiration and ideas when creating sculptural forms. Paul Baliker is the sculptor who created *Fish Story*. He works with wood and bronze, creating sculptures that reflect the wildlife of Florida. *Dark Snapper,* by John Warren, was inspired by the aquatic life of California where he lives. Both artists use free-form forms that they find in nature.

 ## Art History and Culture

Do both of these pieces belong in the same period? Look at the dates in the captions to give you a clue.

▲ **John Warren.**
(American). *Dark Snapper.*
. . . .
Steel and lava rock. 31 inches long
(78.74 cm.).

Study both sculptures to see the use of free-form forms.

▶ What forms do you see in both sculptures?

▶ Describe the shapes in *Dark Snapper*. Are any of these shapes repeated in *Fish Story*? Explain.

▶ Where do you think *Dark Snapper* would best be displayed? Do you think *Fish Story* belongs outdoors? Why?

Aesthetic Perception

Design Awareness Think about outdoor sculptures you may have seen. Where were they? What were they? Did they look like they were part of their environment?

Using Free-Form Forms

Forms are three-dimensional objects measured by height, width, and depth. All forms can be placed into one of two categories: geometric or free-form. **Geometric forms** are forms based on mathematical measurements. **Free-form forms** are three-dimensional; however, they have uneven or irregular edges, like clouds, trees, or rocks have. All human and animal forms are examples of free-form forms. Because free-form forms occur most often in nature, they are sometimes referred to as natural or organic forms.

Practice

Make a list of free-form forms.

1. In a small group, brainstorm a list of free-form forms you have seen.

2. Next to each object on your list, write either an *N* or an *H* (*N* for forms found in nature or *H* for forms made by human hands). There may be some items that fit both categories.

3. Share your list with the class. Add any new ideas to the list.

◀ **Amelia Ankerich.**
Age 11.

Think about how this student artist used free-form forms to create this sculpture model.

🎨 Creative Expression

Create a model for an outdoor sculpture using free-form forms.

1. Look at the sketches you drew in your Art Journal and select one. On sketch paper, make simple contour line drawings of the main forms for your model.

2. Cut a piece of thin wire so that it is about three inches longer than the contour of your drawing. Start at the bottom of the drawing and trace around the object using the wire. Leave about 1½ inches of extra wire at the beginning. As you bend your wire around the line, tape it in place. When you reach the bottom where you started, twist the two ends together so that you form a stake, or stick.

3. Cover your wire shapes with tissue paper.

4. Color your base with acrylic paints. Construct your model by pushing the wire stakes or sticks into the base.

❗ Art Criticism

Describe What materials and forms did you use to create your sculpture? What place or environment did you design your model for?

Analyze Did you use mostly straight or curved lines in the contours of your free-form shapes?

Interpret Based on its subject matter, create a list of all the places your sculpture could be displayed.

Decide Were you able to successfully create a sculpture using free-form shapes and forms for a specific environment? Explain.

Lesson 5

Space and Perspective

▲ **Giovanni Paolo Pannini.** (Italian). *The Picture Gallery of Cardinal Silvio Valenti Gonzaga.* 1749.

Oil on canvas. $78\frac{3}{16} \times 105\frac{3}{8}$ inches (198.6 × 267.67 cm.). Wadsworth Atheneum. Hartford, Connecticut.

Look at how **space** was created in these paintings by giving the illusion of moving back into the canvas. Giovanni Paolo Pannini was the first artist to specialize in painting architectural ruins. In *The Picture Gallery of Cardinal Silvio Valenti Gonzaga,* Pannini allows us to view the cardinal's large collection of art. Vincent van Gogh's *The Café Terrace* was the first work in a trilogy of paintings that had a starlit sky. *Starry Night* and *Portrait of Eugene Boch* were the other two works in the trilogy. This yellow café is still open for business in Arles, France, but it has been renamed Café van Gogh.

Art History and Culture

Are these paintings from the same art movement?

Study both paintings to see how depth is used.

▶ Use your fingers to trace the top of the buildings in van Gogh's painting. Follow the diagonal lines above the arches in Pannini's work. Where do they meet in each painting?

▶ Look at the shapes on the walls and the arched hallway in Pannini's painting. What happens to these shapes the farther away they become? What do you notice about the buildings and tables in van Gogh's painting?

▲ **Vincent van Gogh.** (Dutch).
Café Terrace at Night. 1888.
· ·
Oil on canvas. $31\frac{7}{8} \times 25\frac{13}{16}$ inches (81 × 65.54 cm.).
Kröller-Müller Museum, Otterlo, Netherlands.

Aesthetic Perception

Design Awareness Stand in a long hallway. Look at the lines formed where the walls meet the floor and ceiling on either side of you. As you look down the hallway, what do you notice about these lines?

Space in Two-Dimensional Art

Space is the art element that refers to the areas above, below, between, within, and around an object. In drawings and paintings, artists use perspective techniques to create the illusion of space. **Perspective** is a system used to create the illusion of depth and volume on a flat surface. There are six perspective techniques.

Overlapping: One object covers a portion of another object. The first object appears to be closer and larger.

Size: Objects that are closer look larger than objects that are farther away.

Placement: Objects placed lower in a picture appear to be closer than those placed near eye level. There are three areas on a picture surface: the **foreground,** the area that is closest to the viewer; the **middle ground,** usually toward the center of the picture plane; and the **background,** the area farthest from the viewer.

Detail: Objects with fuzzy, blurred edges appear farther away than those with clear sharp edges.

Color: Bright-colored objects seem closer, while dull or pale objects appear farther away. This is also known as **atmospheric perspective** because the air or atmosphere has an effect on how we see an object.

Converging lines: Parallel lines seem to converge or move toward the same point as they move away from the viewer. This is also known as **linear perspective.**

Practice

Which perspective techniques do you recognize?

1. Look through this book and find eight images you like. Use strips of paper numbered 1 through 8 to mark each image.

2. List the six perspective techniques on a piece of paper.

3. Study each image selected and mark the image number next to each technique that is used. Which technique was used most often?

◄ **Nicole Yackley.**
Age 11.

Think about the perspective techniques used in this student's work.

Creative Expression

Create a **one-point linear perspective** drawing of a hallway in your school.

1. Using a pencil, draw a horizontal or vertical rectangle in the center of your paper, no larger than three inches. This will be the end of the hall. Draw very lightly.

2. Mark a point near the center of your box—the vanishing point. Draw four lines with a ruler coming out from that point toward each corner of your paper. These lines will create the walls of your hallway. Add guide lines for the top and bottom of doors or objects on the walls or in the hall.

3. Outline your drawing with a marker. Erase any unnecessary guide lines. Use watercolor or color pencils, to complete your drawing.

Art Criticism

Describe What objects did you place in your hallway?

Analyze Explain how you used linear perspective.

Interpret Give your work a descriptive title.

Decide Do you feel your linear-perspective drawing was a success? Explain.

Positive and Negative Space

Look at the open areas used in these two sculptures. David Bates assembled various pieces of wood to create *Seated Man #4*. He uses the materials that are available to him from his environment. Spanish artist Pablo Picasso is best known for his cubist paintings and collages of distorted faces and objects. In *Proposal for a Monument to Apollinaire*, Picasso pays tribute to the famous French poet, Guillaume Apollinaire. The completed sculpture in memory of Apollinaire, located in the gardens of the Metropolitan Museum, stands nineteen feet tall.

◀ **David Bates.** (American).
Seated Man #4. 1995.
Painted wood. 88 × 37½ × 45½ inches
(223.52 × 95.25 × 115.57 cm.).
Dallas Museum of Art, Dallas, Texas.

Art History and Culture

What famous sculptures from before the twentieth century are you familiar with?

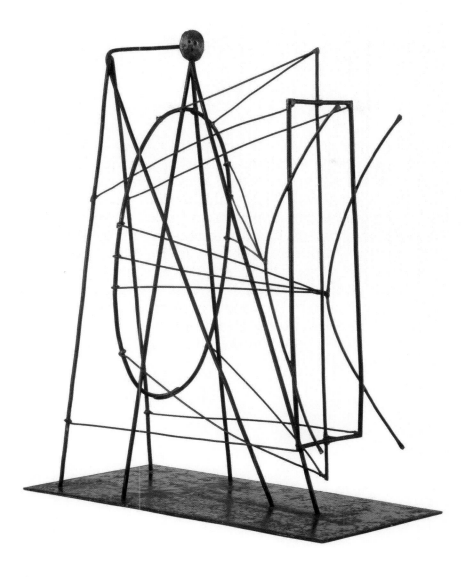

◀ **Pablo Picasso.** (Spanish).
***Proposal for a Monument to
Apollinaire.*** 1928.

Iron and sheet metal. $19\frac{7}{8} \times 7\frac{5}{16} \times 16\frac{1}{16}$ inches
(50.5 × 18.5 × 40.8 cm.). Musée Picasso, Paris,
France.

Study how space is used in three-dimensional sculptures.

▶ Where do you see a large oval in Picasso's sculpture? Describe
this oval.

▶ Look at the lines Picasso used to form the sculpture that honors
Apollinaire. Describe the open spaces between these lines.

▶ What types of shapes do you see in *Seated Man #4*? Describe the
area around these shapes.

▶ Describe the materials used by both artists.

Aesthetic Perception

Seeing Like an Artist Think about a tree with bare branches during the
winter. Describe the empty spaces between, around, above, below, and within
the tree.

Using Positive and Negative Space in Three-Dimensional Art

Space refers to the areas above, below, between, within, and around an object. Space is taken up by all objects. Objects are defined by the area around and within them. In both two- and three-dimensional art, the shapes and forms are called **positive space,** or the figures. The area of empty space between the shapes or forms is called **negative space,** or the ground. In sculpture, both positive and negative spaces are important to understanding the work. Open negative spaces help artists communicate thoughts or feelings in their sculptures. Large negative spaces within a sculpture make it appear to be light and can create feelings of isolation or freedom. The use of little negative space in a sculpture makes it appear to be heavy. It may also make the sculpture appear to be stable and give the feeling of strength or togetherness.

Positive space

Negative space

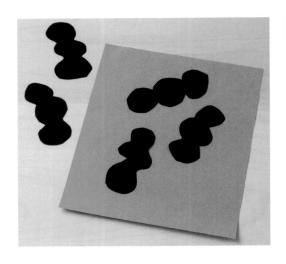

Practice

Use cut shapes to create positive and negative spaces.

1. Cut a sheet of paper into five separate pieces. Each piece should be an ant shape in a different size.

2. On background paper, arrange the cut shapes several times so that you have open spaces between your shapes. Study each of your arrangements.

3. Glue down your best arrangement.

◀ **Galilee Denard.**
Age 12.
Joshua Swift.
Age 11.
Jonathan Tanner.
Age 12.

Think about how these students used both positive and negative space in the sculpture.

 Creative Expression

Construct an **assemblage** using positive and negative space.

1. Look over your selected sketch in your Art Journal. Begin cutting the geometric and free-form shapes for your sculpture. Cut slots and tabs in the shapes to construct your assemblage. Add your features separately, such as eyes, ears, nose, and mouth. Try to create a distinct personality with the facial features.

2. Arrange your shapes on your base as you work. Be sure to include negative space within your sculpture. Glue your sculpture to the base.

3. Use acrylic paints and a marker to add color and details. Glue your collected items to your sculpture to embellish it. Give your completed sculpture a descriptive title.

 **Art Criticism**

Describe How did you create your assemblage? What objects did you add?

Analyze Explain how you arranged your shapes to create positive and negative space in your sculpture.

Interpret Does your sculpture have a personality? Explain.

Decide Do you feel you successfully used positive and negative space in your sculpture? Explain.

▲ **George Bellows.** (American).
Cliff Dwellers. 1913.

Oil on canvas. $40\frac{3}{16} \times 42\frac{1}{16} \times 12$ inches
(102.08 × 106.83 × 30.48 cm.). Los Angeles
County Museum of Art, Los Angeles, California.

Art Criticism | Critical Thinking

Describe What do you see?

During this step you will collect information about the subject of the work.

▶ Describe the objects, the people, and their clothing.

Analyze How is this work organized?

Think about how the artist used the elements and principles of art.

▶ Locate and list the different types of lines.

▶ Where do you see free-form shapes? Where do you see geometric shapes?

▶ How did Bellows show depth?

▶ Is this painting a shape or a form? Explain.

Interpret What is the artist trying to say?

Combine clues you collected during Describe and Analyze with your personal experiences to find out what this painting is about.

▶ Is this a calm or an active picture? Which elements create that feeling?

▶ What did you observe about the time, place, and season in this painting?

Decide What do you think about the work?

Use all the information you have gathered to decide whether this is a successful work of art.

▶ Is this painting successful because it is realistic or well organized? Does it send a message? Explain.

Show What You Know

Answer these questions on a separate sheet of paper.

1 A _____ is a two-dimensional area that is measured by height and width.
  A. shape
  B. space
  C. form

2 The shapes and forms in a work of art represent _____.
  A. geometric forms
  B. converging lines
  C. positive space

3 The area above, below, between, within, and around an object is called _____.
  A. shape
  B. space
  C. form

4 A _____ is the pathway made through space by a moving point.
  A. shape
  B. line
  C. form

5 A chair and a person are examples of _____.
  A. form
  B. perspective
  C. space

CAREERS IN ART
Animation

Think about what cartoons you like. Have you ever wondered how artists get the characters to move? Traditionally, animators created cartoons for movies and television, but now they have more job choices.

Storyboard artists read a movie script and create a storyboard. They visualize the story before they draw it.

Special-effects technicians often work in the movie industry. They work with ordinary images and add computer-generated elements that change the images into fantastic designs.

Layout artists create backgrounds for each scene, usually referring to storyboards and additional research materials. These do not appear in the final product, but are critical for the positioning and perspective of the animation.

▲ **Storyboard Artist**

Line, Shape, Form, and Space in Music and Storytelling

The Robert Minden Ensemble performs musical stories. They turn ordinary objects into musical instruments. In telling the story "The Boy Who Wanted to Talk to Whales," the group uses a carpenter's saw, empty tin cans, wood, vacuum-cleaner hoses, and a spring toy. Conch shells and a microtonal waterphone create a magical ocean sound.

What to Do Listen to and describe ordinary sounds in your environment.

1. Close your eyes. Listen to the sounds in the classroom. Try to visualize the sounds.

2. Write some words or thoughts that describe what you hear when the room is quiet.

3. Take turns reading the descriptions. Discuss what sounds you heard. Did other people hear different sounds? Explain.

4. Repeat the exercise, having different people add sounds to the silence, such as keys jingling, a ruler tapping, or the pages of a book rustling. Listen very carefully. Make a new list of all the sounds you heard.

▲ Robert Minden Ensemble. "The Boy Who Wanted to Talk to Whales."

Art Criticism

Describe Can you describe the sounds in terms of line or shape?

Analyze Explain how the quality, length, and rhythm of the sounds varied.

Interpret How were the sounds alike? How were they different?

Decide Decide whether you were successful in hearing and identifying all the sounds.

Color and Texture

▲ **Auguste Renoir.** (French).
Young Spanish Woman with a Guitar. 1898.
· ·
Oil on canvas. $21\frac{7}{8} \times 25\frac{5}{8}$ inches
(55.6 × 65.2 cm.). National Gallery of Art, Washington, D.C.

Artists use color and texture to create both two- and three-dimensional works of art.

The impressionist artist Auguste Renoir is best known for his paintings of children, outdoor scenes, and beautiful women. His use of color and texture make the people in his portraits seem alive.

Artists use color in all types of artwork.

▶ What colors do you see?

▶ Where are the darkest and lightest colors in this painting?

Artists imitate textures in two-dimensional artwork and use real textures in three-dimensional artwork.

▶ Where do you see rough textures in this painting?

▶ Where do you see smooth textures in this painting?

In This Unit you will learn how artists use color. You will use different color media and processes to create personal works of art. You will also learn about texture you can see and texture you can touch. Here are the topics you will study:
▶ Color spectrum
▶ Color value
▶ Color intensity
▶ Color schemes
▶ Visual texture
▶ Tactile texture

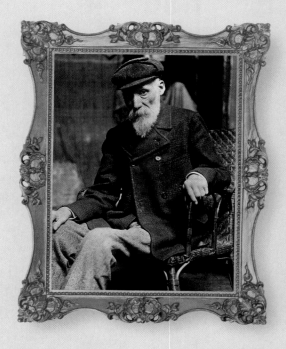

Auguste Renoir
(1841–1919)

Auguste Renoir was born in Limoges, France. He started his career at the age of thirteen as an artist in a porcelain factory. His job was to copy famous paintings of beautiful women onto porcelain plates. This experience taught him how to use color to paint portraits. He later belonged to a group of artists known as impressionists. They were concerned with capturing the impression of light and color in everyday scenes.

Lesson

1 Hue

◀ **Miriam Schapiro.**
(Canadian/American).
Anna and David. 1987.
. . . .
Stainless steel and painted
aluminum. 35 × 31 feet × 6 inches
(10.7 × 9.5 meters × 15.24 cm.).
Rosslyn Metro Station, Arlington,
Virginia.

Look at the two works of art on these pages. Miriam Schapiro
made the sculpture *Anna and David* out of cut steel and
aluminum. These two dancing figures were the subject of a
fabric-and-paint collage created a year earlier. Notice how the
colors look bright against the dark buildings. In *Conception
Synchromy,* Stanton MacDonald-Wright used both primary and
secondary colors. He was interested in exploring how colors react
together. The word *synchromy* means "with color."

Art History and Culture

What is the subject matter of each work of art?

▲ **Stanton MacDonald-Wright.**
(American). *Conception Synchromy.* 1914.

Oil on canvas. 36 × 30⅛ inches
(91.44 × 76.51 cm.). Hirshhorn Museum
and Sculpture Garden, Washington, D.C.

Study both pieces of art to discover more about how artists use color.

▶ What colors do you recognize in both pieces of artwork?

▶ Which color do you see repeated most often in *Anna and David?*

▶ What bright areas of color are next to dark areas in *Anna and David?*

Aesthetic Perception

Design Awareness We are surrounded by different colors. Think about where you have seen a range of colors. Have you seen a rainbow or a prism? What did you notice about the colors?

Using Color

Color is derived from reflected light. Light from the sun is a combination of all colors. When light hits an object, like an apple, you see the color red. The apple absorbs the other colors and reflects the red waves of light, which our brain reads as the hue "red." Hue is another name for color. A wedge-shaped piece of glass called a prism bends light as it passes through. When light bends, the colors separate, creating the color spectrum. The hues in the spectrum always appear in the same order: red, orange, yellow, green, blue, and violet. The color wheel below shows the spectrum bent into a circle.

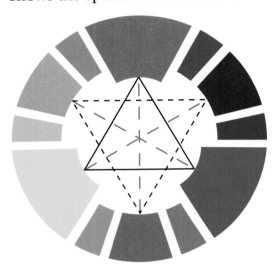

The primary hues —red, yellow, and blue—are used to create the other hues on the color wheel. The primary hues are considered pure colors because they cannot be made by mixing other hues together. When you mix two primary hues you get the secondary hues —orange, green, and violet. When a primary is mixed with an equal amount of a secondary hue an intermediate color is made. For example, yellow and green make yellow-green. Intermediate colors are also called *tertiary colors*.

Practice

As a class, create a color spectrum by lining up students in color order.

1. Look at your clothing and at your classmates' clothing. Begin by finding someone who is wearing the color red. That person will be first in line. Now find the color orange, then yellow, green, blue, and violet.

2. If you are missing a color, have a student hold a piece of construction paper in that color.

3. See if you can come up with ideas on how to create the intermediate colors.

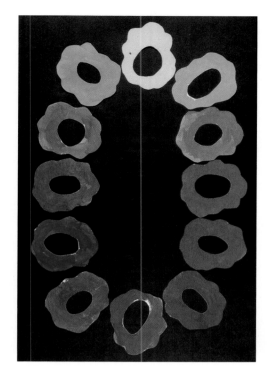

◀ **Ansley Axelberg.**
Age 11.

Think about how this student artist shows the correct color relationships in the color wheel.

Creative Expression

Select any shape or object to create a unique color wheel.

1. Make a pattern of your selected shape or object and trace it twelve times on white paper. Outline your shapes using a permanent marker.

2. Mix only primary colors to make secondary and intermediate colors. Paint your first three shapes the primary colors. Paint the next three shapes the secondary colors. Paint the last shapes the intermediate colors.

3. Once your shapes are dry, cut them out. Arrange them to show the correct color relationships. Your color wheel does not have to be perfectly round, nor does it have to be a wheel. Glue your shapes onto a black or white background once you have your idea.

Art Criticism

Describe What shape or object did you use? How did you arrange your color wheel?

Analyze Describe how you made each of your intermediate colors.

Interpret Describe how someone would read your color wheel.

Decide Do you feel you were able to create a unique color wheel that shows the correct color relationships? Explain.

Value

▲ **Vincent van Gogh.** (Dutch).
Portrait of Joseph Roulin. 1888.

Reed and quill pen, brown ink, and black chalk. $12\frac{5}{8} \times 9\frac{5}{8}$ inches
(32.06 × 24.44 cm.). The J. Paul Getty Museum, Los Angeles, California.

Look at the two works of art on these pages. Vincent van Gogh drew *Portrait of Joseph Roulin,* an image of the local postmaster. Van Gogh wrote almost daily to his brother, and so he became friends with Roulin. He created many drawings and paintings of the Roulin family. John Henry Twachtman painted images that reflected the changing seasons at his home in Greenwich, Connecticut. He is considered an American impressionist painter. The landscape *Snow Scene* captures the effects of light and atmosphere on a common subject. Notice how shadows and highlights are created differently in both works of art.

 ## Art History and Culture

Which other artists created portraits or landscapes?

▲ **John Henry Twachtman.**
(American). *Snow Scene.*
1882.

Oil on canvas. $12\frac{1}{16} \times 16\frac{1}{16}$ inches
(30.63 × 40.79 cm.). Cincinnati Art
Museum, Cincinnati, Ohio.

Study both works of art to see how the artists used
shadow and light in their artwork.

▶ Find the light and dark areas in *Snow Scene*. Do you
see a gradual change in the painting from light to dark?

▶ Describe how Vincent van Gogh depicted dark and
light areas in his drawing of Joseph Roulin.

▶ What direction are the light sources coming from in
these two pieces of art?

▶ What mood is created by the light and shadows in each
work of art?

🔍 Aesthetic Perception

Design Awareness Think about the shadows you see in the early morning
or at the end of the day. How are they different from the shadows at noon or
midday? How do the shadows differ on a sunny day versus a cloudy day?

Using Value

Value refers to the darkness or lightness of a hue. Not all hues have the same value; yellow has the lightest value and violet has the darkest. **Neutral colors** —black, gray, and white—can be added to any hue to change its value. The more black that is added to a color, the darker the hue; the more white, the lighter the hue.

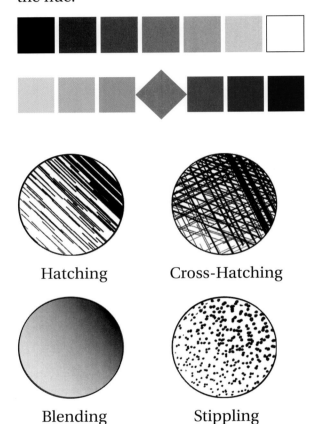

A light value of a hue is called a **tint.** It is made by adding white to a hue. The more white that is added to a hue, the lighter the tint or value. Add black to a hue to make a dark value called a **shade.** A color scheme that is made of one hue and the tints and shades of that hue is a monochromatic color scheme.

Hatching   Cross-Hatching

Blending   Stippling

When drawing, artists often use the shading techniques hatching, cross-hatching, blending, and stippling. **Hatching** is a series of parallel lines. **Cross-hatching** is sets of parallel lines that cross or intersect. **Blending** is a gradual change from light to dark or dark to light. **Stippling** uses dots; the closer the dots, the darker the value.

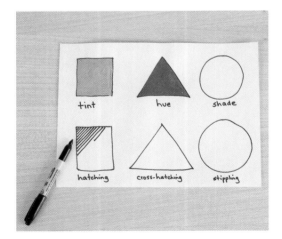

Practice

Practice shading techniques. Use tempera paint and a fine-tipped marker.

1. Draw two horizontal rows of three shapes each. Label the shapes on the first row *tint, hue,* and *shade.* Label the remaining shapes *hatching, cross-hatching,* and *stippling.*

2. Choose a primary color and paint in the "hue" shape. Mix white with your hue to create a tint. Next, mix black to create a shade of your hue.

3. Look at the figure above and imitate the shading techniques to complete the second row of shapes.

◄ **Alexx Diera.**
Age 13.

Think about this painting. What monochromatic colors did the student artist use?

 **Creative Expression**

Paint a landscape using monochromatic colors to show value.

1. Look over your planned sketch in your Art Journal. Lightly transfer your sketch onto your paper, filling the whole page.

2. Select any one color from the color wheel. From your paint palette, mix tints and shades and try them out on a scrap sheet of paper.

3. Paint your landscapes. Using tints and shades of your selected color, make gradual changes in value in some areas of your painting. Show a wide range of values from almost-white highlights to dark shadows.

Art Criticism

Describe What is in your landscape?

Analyze Describe your monochromatic color scheme. Explain how you created a range of values.

Interpret How does the value change affect the mood?

Decide Were you successful in creating a monochromatic painting with a wide range of values? Explain.

Intensity

▲ **André Derain.** (French). *Portrait of a Young Girl in Black.* 1914.

Oil on canvas. 45 × 34½ inches (114.3 × 87.63 cm.). State Hermitage Museum, St. Petersburg, Russia.

Look at how both portraits were painted using color intensity. Derain used a range of values when painting *Portrait of a Young Girl in Black.* He is best known for creating brightly colored landscapes and cityscapes. Schmidt-Rottluff was interested in the simple shapes and distorted features of African masks. He helped form a group that he named *Die Brücke,* or "The Bridge." The group believed that they were the bridge between traditional and modern art. In *Portrait of Emy,* Schmidt-Rottluff uses the bright colors characteristic of *Die Brücke.* Emy was his wife.

Art History and Culture

Were Derain and Schmidt-Rotluff contemporaries?

▲ **Karl Schmidt-Rottluff.**
(German). *Portrait of Emy.* 1919.

Oil on canvas. $28\frac{5}{16} \times 25\frac{3}{4}$ inches
(71.91 × 65.41 cm.). North Carolina
Museum of Art, Raleigh, North Carolina.

Study both portraits on these pages. How did the artists use color in their paintings?

▶ What colors do you see?

▶ Describe the different values used in each painting.

▶ Which color dominates the painting *Portrait of a Young Girl in Black?* Why do you think Derain chose this color?

▶ How was contrast used in *Portrait of Emy* by Karl Schmidt-Rottluff?

Aesthetic Perception

Seeing Like an Artist What colors do you think of when you imagine the bark of a tree?

Using Intensity

Intensity is the brightness or dullness of a color. A pure hue is called a high-intensity color. Dull hues are called low-intensity colors. One way to create a low-intensity color is to mix a color with its complement.

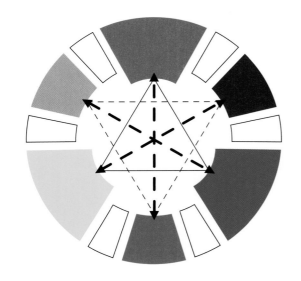

Complementary colors are colors that are opposite each other on the color wheel. For example, blue and orange are complementary colors. The complement of a hue absorbs all the light waves that the hue reflects. It is the strongest contrast to that color. For example, orange absorbs blue waves and reflects yellow and red waves. Yellow and red combine to make orange.

Mixing a hue with its complementary color dulls it. It lowers the intensity. The more of the complement you add, the duller the hue becomes. Eventually the hue will lose its own color and become a neutral gray or brownish color.

Practice

Practice mixing low-intensity colors.

1. Draw a rectangle large enough to fill your paper. Divide it into five sections.

2. Look at the color wheel, and select one set of complementary colors.

3. Look at the intensity scale. Begin by coloring your first shape one hue and the last shape its complement. Color the next shape in from both sides the pure hue and mix a little of its complement. The center shape will have equal amounts of both complementary colors, creating a neutral gray or brown.

◀ **Chandler Verner.**
Age 11.

Think about the portrait created by the student artist. Can you tell what complements were used to create the high- and low-intensity colors?

 Creative Expression

Make an oil pastel portrait using bright and dull colors to create a mood.

1. Choose your best sketch from your Art Journal. Transfer it onto your paper, touching three edges to fill your page.

2. Select any one complementary color set. On a scrap sheet of paper, practice blending colors and creating textures.

3. Color in your portrait with oil pastels. Overlap and blend colors in some areas of your work; use bright colors in other areas. Show both high- and low-intensity colors. Keep your background simple so that it does not distract from the portrait.

 Art Criticism

Describe Who is the person in your drawing? What oil pastel techniques did you use?

Analyze Describe your complementary color scheme. How did you create low- and high-intensity colors?

Interpret How do the colors affect the mood?

Decide Were you successful in creating a portrait using low- and high-intensity colors? Explain.

Color Schemes

▲ **James Ensor.** (Belgian).
Fireworks. 1887.

Oil and encaustic on canvas.
$40\frac{1}{4} \times 44\frac{1}{4}$ inches (102.24 × 112.4 cm.).
Albright-Knox Art Gallery, Buffalo,
New York.

Look at how Ensor used complementary colors to draw your attention away from the dark ground in *Fireworks.* By applying pigment to wash, he created a thick paint called *impasto.* This paint adds to the texture of his painting. Georges Braque used low-intensity and neutral colors in *Fishing Boats.* Braque and Pablo Picasso invented the style of art called *cubism.* This style emphasizes structure and design. Notice how the objects are shown from different points of view at the same time.

 Art History and Culture

Did you know that Ensor was a founding member of the group *Les XX,* and that Braque co-founded cubism?

▲ **Georges Braque.** (French).
Fishing Boats. 1909.
....
Oil on canvas. $36\frac{1}{4} \times 28\frac{7}{8}$ inches
(92.08 × 73.36 cm.). Museum of
Fine Arts, Houston, Texas.

Study and compare how the artists used different color schemes in their paintings.

► List the objects you see in each painting.

► What colors are used in *Fireworks?* What colors are used in *Fishing Boats?*

► Which color do you notice first in *Fireworks?* Why do you think this happens?

► Which areas are the lightest and darkest in each painting?

Aesthetic Perception

Design Awareness Look at the clothing you and your classmates are wearing. Which colors would "go together" or look good? Which colors would contrast?

Using Color Schemes

A **color scheme** is a plan for organizing the colors used in an artwork. When two colors come into contact, their differences increase. Some colors look good together, while others clash. Artists use color schemes to help them organize colors so that they can communicate an idea or an emotion. Primary, secondary, intermediate, monochromatic, and complementary colors are color schemes that have already been discussed in this unit, but there are two other color schemes that are used frequently.

Analogous colors are colors that sit side by side on the color wheel and have a common hue. Violet, blue-violet, blue, blue-green, and green all have blue in common. You can narrow this related scheme by limiting it to only three colors, such as violet, blue-violet, and blue.

The color spectrum is divided into two groups—warm colors and cool colors, which are associated with temperature. **Warm colors** are red, yellow, and orange and suggest warmth. **Cool colors** are violet, blue, and green and suggest coolness. Warm colors seem to move toward the viewer, and cool colors seem to recede or go back from the viewer.

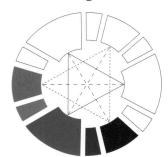

Analogous colors

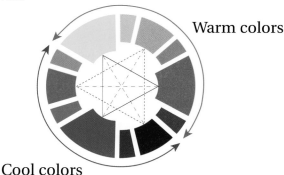

Warm colors

Cool colors

Practice

Look through magazines to find pictures that illustrate different color schemes.

1. As a table group, find at least one example of each color scheme in your magazines.

2. On self-adhesive notes write each of the color scheme names as you find them to label your examples. Tag the pages with the adhesive notes.

3. Do not tear out the pages. See how many examples you can find.

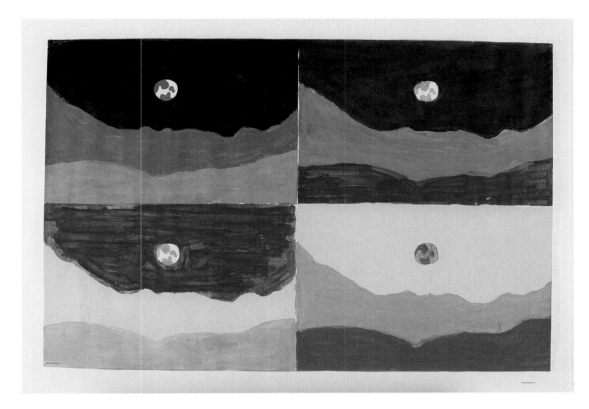

◀ **Janet Becker.**
Age 11.

Think about the landscape created by the student artist. Do you recognize the four color schemes used?

 **Creative Expression**

Use different color schemes to paint a series of four similar landscapes.

1. Divide your paper into four equal sections. Fold the paper in half, open it, and fold it in half in the opposite direction.

2. Using your sketch, make a simple line drawing on a small piece of paper. Transfer your line drawing onto each of the rectangles on your drawing paper.

3. Look at the color schemes in this unit, and select any four. Paint each of your four small landscapes, using a different color scheme.

4. Use the primary and secondary colors to mix your intermediate colors. Using a small brush, paint the shapes by outlining them with a color. Then use a medium-sized brush to fill them in.

Art Criticism

Describe List all the objects in your landscapes.

Analyze Describe the four different color schemes you used.

Interpret Compare how the different color schemes affect the mood in each landscape.

Decide Were you successful in creating a series of four landscapes using different color schemes? Explain.

Visual Texture

▲ **Susan LeVan.** (American).
Two Birds in Hand.

Digital media. Bruck & Moss Gallery,
New York, New York.

Look closely at the works of art by LeVan and Chardin. Notice how these artists used lines and value to show smooth and bumpy areas. Chardin used thick layers of color and thin glazes to create the feeling of smooth, rough, matte, and shiny surfaces. *Still Life with the Attributes of the Arts* has objects that represent the arts. The paintbrushes represent painting, and the statue is of Mercury, the god of the arts. Susan LeVan created *Two Birds in Hand* on a computer. She uses a program that allows her to alter colors so that she can imitate rough and smooth surfaces. Though these artists are from two different centuries, they both understood how to imitate different surfaces.

Art History and Culture

Which of these two works of art was created in the twentieth century?

▲ **Jean-Baptiste Simeon Chardin.**
(French). *Still Life with the Attributes of the Arts.* 1766.

Oil on canvas. 44 × 55 inches (111.76 × 139.7 cm.).
State Hermitage Museum, St. Petersburg, Russia.

Study both works of art to see how visual texture is used.

▶ Where do you see a bumpy surface?

▶ Look closely at the painting by Chardin. List the objects that are rough, smooth, matte, or shiny.

▶ Which area in LeVan's picture looks smooth?

▶ Describe the surface area of the shirt in LeVan's picture.

Aesthetic Perception

Design Awareness Think about the following items: an egg, a feather, a leather coat, and the chrome on a car. How does light reflect or shine on these surfaces?

Using Visual Texture

Everything has texture. **Texture** refers to how things feel, or how things look as if they might feel if touched.

You perceive texture with two of your senses: touch and sight. When you look at a surface, you can guess how it would feel. This is based on prior experiences of touching that surface or a similar surface. Your eyes communicate with your brain how an object would feel if you were to touch it.

When you look at photographs of objects, the lights and shadows create surface patterns that imitate texture. This is called **visual texture,** or the illusion of a three-dimensional surface. Another name for visual texture is *simulated texture.* **Simulated texture** imitates real textures. Plastic surfaces that look like real wood, and material made to look like real leather are examples of simulated textures. Artists use simulated textures to imitate textures that are rough, smooth, matte, or shiny.

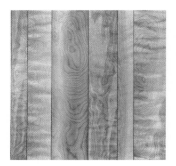   

Simulated textures   Real textures

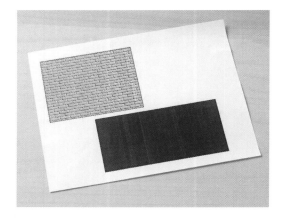

Practice

Use a computer to experiment with visual texture.

1. Use a photo-editing program to explore textures.

2. Open the document your teacher has prepared. Select the menu to see the choices you have. Fill in the shapes with textures that interest you.

3. Print a copy of the textures and label them to use for reference.

◀ **Katie C. Fetzer.**
Age 10.

Think about the types of textures you recognize in this student's work.

 Creative Expression

Explore using the computer as an art tool for creating textured drawings.

1. Look over your sketch and draw your image using a computer program. Use any tools or options available on your software to resize and manipulate the image. When your image is completed to your satisfaction, save it as "Original Image."

2. Copy your image and save it as "Drawing 1." Use the fill bucket and other tools to add and create textures.

3. Copy several images and explore a variety of textures for each one. Label and save each drawing as you complete it.

4. Select your three best images to print.

 **Art Criticism**

Describe Describe your original image. Describe your favorite image.

Analyze List the different textures you were able to create.

Interpret Compare how the various textures used in your drawings alter the images.

Decide Which of your computer drawings do you feel best portrays visual texture? Explain.

Lesson 6 Tactile Texture

Look at the two headpieces on these pages. *King's Crown* is an image of a headpiece worn during a ceremony to celebrate a new king. The long beads are not to keep people from looking at the new chief, but to partially block the chief's view so that he is forced to look within himself. This keeps him from being distracted by what is going on around him during the time of this ceremony. *Coming of Age Hat* was also created for the purpose of ceremony. It is given to a boy when he turns twelve. It represents leaving childhood and becoming a young adult. The objects attached all have personal meaning for the young boy who receives the hat. If you look closely at the circle in the center of the brim you will see an embroidered image of the boy who owned this hat. Both of these headpieces are made of a variety of textured materials and objects.

◀ **Artist unknown.** (Yoruba). *King's Crash.* c. 1930.

Bamboo framework, beads, cloth, leather. 12-inch diameter (30.48 cm.). Saint Louis Museum of Art, Saint Louis, Missouri.

 Art History and Culture

Did you know that the origin of hats can be traced back to primitive humans?

▲ **Artist unknown.** (Chinese).
Coming of Age Hat.
Twentieth century.
....
Mixed media, embroidery. 12 × 15 inches
(30.48 × 38.1 cm). Private Collection.

Study how tactile texture is used in these three-dimensional forms.

▶ Where do you see a face? Describe the materials used.

▶ Look closely at both headpieces. List the objects that are rough, smooth, matte, or shiny.

▶ List the materials used by both artists.

Aesthetic Perception

Design Awareness Think about hats that you or someone you know may have worn to celebrate an event. What were they like? Can you think of any cultures today that use headpieces for ceremonies or celebrations?

Using Tactile Texture

Tactile textures, or actual textures, are textures you can touch and feel. When light reflects off a surface, it displays a pattern of light and dark values. From this pattern we can make a judgment about the texture of a surface or object, even if we cannot touch it.

There are four basic types of texture: rough, smooth, shiny, and matte. Sometimes these textures are combined, such as shiny-smooth or matte-smooth.

Rough-textured surfaces reflect light unevenly. They show irregular patterns of light and dark.

Smooth-textured surfaces reflect light evenly. They have no dents and so no patterns of light or shadows appear.

Shiny-textured surfaces reflect bright light. They have highlights and sometimes reflect bright sunlight that makes you squint your eyes.

Matte-textured surfaces reflect light that is soft, with an almost dull look.

Artists often use a variety of tactile textures when creating three-dimensional forms. They sometimes combine more than one material or medium, such as beads, fabric, wood, and metal. This type of art, in which an art object is created from an assortment of media, is called **mixed-media.**

Practice

Look in magazines for images of the four textures: smooth, rough, shiny, and matte.

1. Fold a sheet of paper into four sections.

2. Label each section with one of the four textures.

3. Look through a magazine for examples of each texture and cut them out. Glue each example in its proper box.

◀ **Paden Janney.**
Age 10.

Think about how this student artist used tactile textures in the celebratory hat.

Creative Expression

Create a mixed-media celebratory hat using tactile textures.

1. Look over your ideas in your Art Journal. Bring in an old hat to decorate, or make a headpiece from decorated paper. Place collected textured items in a central location to be shared. Keep your personal objects in a separate envelope or bag.

2. Begin by decorating your hat with various real textures, such as beads, ribbon, lace, and fabric. Overlap some of the material, and use thread, yarn, and glue to attach it to your hat base.

3. Next think about how your personal objects will be arranged to convey the theme of your chosen event or memory. Use thread, yarn, and glue to attach your items to your hat.

Art Criticism

Describe How did you create your hat? What objects did you add?

Analyze Describe the different textures you used in your celebratory hat.

Interpret What event or memory does your hat represent?

Decide Do you feel you successfully used tactile textures in your celebratory hat? Explain why or why not.

Color and Texture

▲ **Mary Cassatt.** (American).
Mother and Child. c. 1890.

Oil on canvas. $35\frac{3}{8} \times 25\frac{3}{8}$ inches (89.87 × 64.47 cm.).
Wichita Museum, Wichita, Kansas.

Art Criticism | Critical Thinking

Describe What do you see?

During this step you will collect information about the subject of the work.

► List and describe the people, their posture, and their clothing.

► Describe what you see in the background.

Analyze How is this work organized?

Think about how the artist used the elements and principles of art.

► Which hues do you see? Where are they?

► Where are the darkest values? Where are the lightest values?

► Where do you see realistic visual texture? Where do you see tactile texture?

Interpret What is the artist trying to say?

Combine clues you collected during description and analysis with your personal experiences to find out what this painting is about.

► What does this work tell you about the relationship between the woman and the child?

► What do the clothing and background tell you about the time this was painted?

► What emotion does this work convey?

Decide What do you think about the work?

Use all the information you have gathered to decide why this is a successful work of art.

► Is this painting successful because it is realistic, well organized, and conveys a message? Explain.

Color and Texture, continued

Show What You Know

Answer these questions on a separate sheet of paper.

❶ _____ is the brightness or dullness of a color.
  A. Tint
  B. Stippling
  C. Intensity

❷ _____ refers to how things feel, or how they look as they might feel, if touched.
  A. Texture
  B. Hue
  C. Color wheel

❸ Red, blue, and yellow are _____.
  A. intermediate colors
  B. primary colors
  C. secondary colors

❹ _____ refers to the darkness and lightness of a hue.
  A. Shade
  B. Hatching
  C. Value

❺ A _____ is a plan for organizing the colors used in an artwork.
  A. color scheme
  B. visual texture
  C. neutral color

VISIT A MUSEUM
The Whitney Museum

The Whitney Museum in New York, New York, is home to one of the world's best collections of twentieth-century American art. The permanent collection at the Whitney contains about 12,000 works, including paintings, sculptures, prints, drawings, and photographs. The museum was founded in 1931 with 700 pieces, many of them from the personal collection of founder Gertrude Vanderbilt Whitney. Today, the Whitney has works of art by nearly 2,000 artists and holds the world's largest collection of works by Edward Hopper, Alexander Calder, and Reginald Marsh. The museum also has major holdings by Marsden Hartley, Georgia O'Keeffe, Charles Burchfield, Gaston Lachaise, Louise Nevelson, and Agnes Martin.

Color and Texture in Dance

"Sarve Kashmir" is a joyous Persian dance. The dancer's jewelry add rhythmic texture to the music. The intense colors and shiny texture of the costumes are similar to those found in the deserts of Northern Africa. The women wear open veils over their heads to shield them from the hot sun.

What to Do Create a musical hand-rattle from simple found materials.

1. Collect bottle caps (about ten per person). Make a hole in the center of each one that is larger than the width of an unsharpened pencil.

2. Thread two, back to back bottle caps, onto a stick until you have five sets. After they are on the stick, bind each end of the stick. Leave enough space for them to rattle against each other. You need enough room for the caps to move up and down so they can make noise. Make sure you leave enough room on one end to hold it as you shake.

3. Use masking tape or raffia to bind the end or glue a large wooden bead on each end. Decorate your hand rattle with pieces of colored raffia or other decorative material.

4. Put on a lively piece of music and use your rattle to emphasize the basic beat or create a rhythm pattern that works well musically.

▲ Djanbazian Dance Company. "Sarve Kashmir."

Describe Can you describe the texture of the rattle sounds?

Analyze Explain how the sharp, percussive sounds of the music could be shown visually using texture and color.

Interpret Is there a variety in the pitch of the sounds of different instruments or do they all sound the same? How could this be used with dance?

Decide Decide whether you were successful making a musical rattle.

Rhythm, Movement, and Pattern

▲ **Max Weber.** (American).
Chinese Restaurant. 1915.

Oil on canvas. 40 × 48 inches
(101.6 × 121.92 cm.). Whitney
Museum of American Art, New York,
New York.

Artists use pattern, rhythm, and movement to arrange the art elements in all kinds of artwork.

American artist Max Weber was best known for introducing cubism and modern art to the United States. Cubism was developed by Pablo Picasso and Georges Braque. This style of art broke down three-dimensional objects into flat shapes which were arranged so that all sides could be seen at once. In *Chinese Restaurant,* Weber uses the elements of cubism. The top and side of the table can be seen at the same time.

Artists use **pattern** in all types of artwork.

▶ What repeated lines and shapes do you see? Describe these lines.

Artists use **rhythm** in two-dimensional artwork to organize the art elements and objects.

▶ What art elements do you see repeated?

▶ Which element attracts your eye most: line, shape, or color? Explain.

Movement is used to move the viewer's eyes in an artwork by placing the art elements or objects in a certain order.

▶ Which elements or objects are pulling your eyes through the artwork?

In This Unit you will learn about how artists create and use pattern. Art elements and objects create a motif that, when repeated, create different types of patterns. You will also learn about rhythm, the illusion of movement, and movement that you actually can see.

Here are the topics you will study:
▶ Pattern
▶ Motif
▶ Random pattern
▶ Regular pattern
▶ Alternating pattern
▶ Three-dimensional pattern
▶ Rhythm
▶ Movement
▶ Visual movement
▶ Kinetic movement

Max Weber
(1881–1961)

Max Weber was born in Bialystok, Russia, and came to the United States at the age of ten. In 1909 he went to Paris to study art. There he met Pablo Picasso, Georges Braque, Paul Cézanne, and Henri Matisse. The works of these artists all shaped Weber's style and influenced his subject matter. He worked in the style of cubism, breaking down objects into their basic shapes in the manner of Picasso and Braque. Weber used bright colors in his work, like Matisse, and created space through overlapping of shapes, like Cézanne. After 1920 Weber developed a more realistic style.

Motif and Pattern

▲ **Artist unknown.** (Kwakwaka'wakw).
Face Mask of Ḵumugwe'. c. 1880.
••
Alder, red cedar bark, cloth, paint. 19¼ × 17 × 6 inches
(48.9 × 43.18 × 15.24 cm.). Hauberg Collection,
Seattle Museum of Art, Seattle, Washington.

Look at the two works of art on these pages. *Face Mask of Ḵumugwe'* was carved from wood and painted in the traditional colors of blue, white, red, and black. This mask was used in a day-long ceremony and worn by a dancer who represented the chief of the undersea creatures. *Egungun from Ogbomoso* is part of a costume used to honor ancestors during the egungun ("powers concealed") ceremony. Each costume is made of layers of cloth in a variety of colors, textures, and patterns. The fabric strips are attached to a wood panel that is balanced on top of the head. Each year the family member who wears the costume adds new strips of valuable cloth. Notice how the colors and shapes are repeated in both works of art.

 **Art History and Culture**

Do you think that these costumes are from the same culture?

▲ **Artist unknown.** (Yoruba).
Egungun from Ogbomoso.
Twentieth century.

Cloth, wood, buttons. Approximately 60
inches (152.4 cm.). North Carolina
Museum of Art, Raleigh, North Carolina.

Study both pieces of art to discover more about how artists use motif and pattern.

▶ What colors, lines, and shapes do you recognize in both pieces of art?

▶ Which color, line, and shape are repeated most often in *Face Mask of Kumugwe'*?

▶ Look closely at *Egungun from Ogbomoso.* Describe any two strips of fabric that show repeated lines, shapes, and colors.

Aesthetic Perception

Seeing Like an Artist We are surrounded by different patterns. Think about a tree or plant you have seen. What shape are the leaves? Are all the leaves on the tree or plant basically the same?

Using Motif and Pattern

When people think of a pattern they think of something that is repeated. In art this "something" is called a motif. A **motif** is an object or art element that is repeated. Each motif is an exact duplicate of the first. For example, in a striped shirt, the first set of stripes is a motif. When a motif, like the stripe on a shirt, is repeated, a pattern is created. A **pattern** is a repeated surface decoration. The motif is the unit of repetition in the pattern.

These are the motifs of the two patterns above.

Practice

Design a motif using color, line, and shape.

1. Fold a piece of paper into four sections. Using your pencil, draw a different motif in each section.

2. Draw one motif using only black and white, draw a second using straight lines, and use a free-form shape in the third. In your fourth section create a motif of your choice. Use color pencils to complete.

◀ **Tiffany Fauvre.**
Age 11.

Think about and describe the motif and pattern this student artist used in the costume design.

 **Creative Expression**

Use two or more motifs to create patterns for a costume design for an event.

1. Begin by lightly drawing two or more figures dressed in costume. Refer to your sketches and the student's art above.

2. Look at the motifs you created in the Practice activity. Select one of these to begin a pattern in part of one of the costumes or create a new one. Use a ruler to help you draw straight lines.

3. Continue creating patterns based on your motifs. You may use the same motif again, but change the color.

4. Once your drawing is complete, outline it using a fine-line black marker. Use either color pencils or markers to finish your work.

Art Criticism

Describe How many people are included in your drawing?

Analyze Describe how you made each of your patterns.

Interpret Could someone guess which event your costumed figures would be a part of based on the patterns? Explain.

Decide Do you feel you were able to successfully create patterns based on different motifs? Explain.

Lesson 2

Two-Dimensional Pattern

Look at the two works of art on these pages. Marsden Hartley painted *Indian Fantasy* with oil paints. Hartley created a series of what he called "the idea of America" in 1914. This series consisted of four paintings showing his interpretations. Minnie Evans used color pencils to create *King*. Her drawings and paintings reflect her private dreams. It is believed that the floral motifs she uses in her artwork were inspired by the Airlie Gardens in North Carolina. She worked as a gatekeeper for more than 25 years at the gardens. Notice how the repeated patterns are created using colors, lines, and shapes.

▲ **Marsden Hartley.** (American).
Indian Fantasy. 1914.

Oil on canvas. $46\frac{11}{16} \times 39\frac{5}{16}$ inches
(118.59 × 99.95 cm.). North Carolina
Museum of Art, Raleigh, North Carolina.

Art History and Culture

Can you tell which of these artists was self-taught?

Study both pieces of art to discover more about how artists use different types of patterns in their artwork.

► Which color, line, shape, or object is repeated most often in *Indian Fantasy*?

► Which color, line, shape, or object is repeated most often in *King*?

► Describe how the motifs are arranged in each artwork.

▲ **Minnie Evans.** (American).
King. 1962.

Colored pencil on paper. $11\frac{7}{8} \times 8\frac{3}{4}$ inches (30.18 × 22.23 cm.). North Carolina Museum of Art, Raleigh, North Carolina.

Aesthetic Perception

Design Awareness Think about where you live. What does the outside of your home look like? What motif is used most often and how is it arranged?

Using Pattern Types

You have learned that a **pattern** is a repeated surface decoration. The unit of repetition in the pattern is called a **motif.** Each motif is an exact duplicate of the first unit. When a motif is repeated, a pattern is created. How the motif is arranged can be grouped into one of three different types of patterns: random, alternating, and regular.

A **random pattern** occurs when the motif is repeated in no apparent order. For example, the leaves that cover the ground during autumn form a random pattern.

A **regular pattern** occurs when the motif is repeated with an equal amount of space between each unit. Regular patterns have a sense of order. For example, the lines indicating parking spaces and the windows in skyscrapers create regular patterns.

An **alternating pattern** can occur in three ways. It can repeat a motif but change position, alter spacing between motifs, or add a second motif. Bricks and stones are often laid in alternating patterns.

Practice

Practice the three pattern types. Use geometric shapes.

1. Look at the pattern types defined above. Fold your paper into four sections. Label each section with a pattern type. Leave the last section blank.

2. Using your pencil, draw simple geometric shapes to create random, regular, and alternating patterns in each section.

3. In the last section, combine two of the pattern types. Label this section with the two pattern types that you used.

◀ **Alexandrea Brandl.**
Age 11.

Think about the types of patterns used by this student artist in the pattern design.

Creative Expression

Use all three pattern types to create a nonobjective design.

1. Begin by lightly drawing one large shape off center on your paper. Divide the rest of your paper using straight and curved lines. Have your lines go through your shape. You will have created a variety of shapes.

2. Look at the patterns you created in the Practice activity. Select one of these to begin a pattern in one of the shapes in your design or create a new one. Use a ruler to help you draw straight lines.

3. Continue creating patterns in each shape. Use random, regular, and alternating patterns.

4. Use either color pencils or markers to finish your patterns and complete your work.

Art Criticism

Describe What shape did you use to begin your design?

Analyze Describe the patterns and colors in your work.

Interpret If you could put a beat to your work, how would it sound?

Decide Do you feel you were able to successfully create the different types of patterns in a nonobjective drawing? Explain.

Three-Dimensional Pattern

▲ **Teodora Blanco.** (Mexican). *Ceramic Figures.* 1978.

Single-fired earthenware. Average height 14 inches (35.56 cm.). Nelson A. Rockefeller Collection, San Antonio Museum of Art, Texas.

Look at the sculptures on these pages. Teodora Blanco is considered one of the most important folk artists of Mexico. She uses surface designs and patterns that make her sculptures unique. The Oaxacan sculptures are carved by the Zapotec people, who still live in the southern Mexican state of Oaxaca. The sculptures are hand-painted, then decorated with tiny detailed patterns. The most popular images are of animals, mystical beasts, and religious figures.

 Art History and Culture

Folk artists usually use traditional techniques and styles of a particular region that have been used for many generations.

Study the sculptures on these pages. How did the artists use patterns in their work?

▶ What objects do you see in *Ceramic Figures?*

▶ Describe the art elements used most often to decorate the surface of the Oaxacan sculptures.

▶ Describe how the patterns were applied to the Oaxacan sculptures and *Ceramic Figures.*

▲ **Artist unknown.**
(Oaxacan, Mexican).
Carved Animals.
. . . .
Private collection.

Aesthetic Perception

Design Awareness What patterns do you see in the clothing around you? What patterns do you see in the fur of an animal?

Using Three-Dimensional Pattern

A **pattern** is a repeated surface decoration. There are three types of patterns: regular, random, and alternating. The motif is the unit of repetition in a pattern. In both two- and three-dimensional artwork, artists use the same types of patterns. They also create them the same way—by repeating a motif.

In three-dimensional art, there are different ways an artist can create a pattern on a form's surface. An artist can create a pattern on clay by gently pressing an object or stamp into the clay surface. Patterns can be drawn using a clay needle, pencil, or other sharp tool. Clay forms and coils can be used to create raised patterns. In all sculptural forms, patterns can be added by drawing and painting or by adding similar objects to the surface.

Practice

Practice drawing random, regular, and alternating patterns using oil pastels.

1. Select three different colors of construction paper.

2. Use oil pastels in a contrasting color to create a random pattern using a motif. On a second piece of construction paper, draw a regular pattern. Create an alternating pattern on a third piece of colored construction paper.

3. Look at the three pattern types you created. How could these be used on a three-dimensional form?

◀ **Harley Dean.**
Age 11.

Think about the types of designs that were applied to the surface of the animal form.

 **Creative Expression**

Form a three-dimensional real or fantasy animal covered with patterns.

1. Begin by forming your clay animal.

2. Once you have your basic animal form, add ears. You can either pinch out or attach the ear forms.

3. Think about other details that are important for your particular animal, like eyes and feet. When you have finished forming your animal, use a toothpick or pencil to add details.

4. Paint your animal using one or two base colors. Once the base color has dried, add patterns using a thin brush or paint pen. Dots and lines can be layered on top of one another.

Art Criticism

Describe What animal did you create?

Analyze Describe the patterns and colors you used.

Interpret What effect do the pattern and color have on your animal sculpture?

Decide Were you successful in creating a three-dimensional real or fantasy animal covered with patterns? Explain.

Rhythm

Look at the artwork on these pages. The repetition of shapes and colors create rhythm in *Animals in Landscape.* The blues pull the eye to the right side; the greens dance across the bottom. The warm colors pull the viewer's eyes down from the upper left and into the work. Pablo Picasso developed the style known as cubism. *Portrait of Dora Maar* is an example of cubism, which portrays a three-dimensional object from many viewpoints at once.

▲ **Franz Marc.** (German). *Animals in a Landscape.* 1914.

Oil on canvas. $43\frac{3}{8} \times 39\frac{1}{4}$ inches (110.2 × 99.7 cm.). Detroit Institute of Arts, Detroit, Michigan.

 Art History and Culture

Are Pablo Picasso and Franz Marc part of the modern art movement?

▲ **Pablo Picasso.** (Spanish).
Portrait of Dora Maar. 1938.

Pencil on paper mounted on fiberboard. $30\frac{9}{16} \times 22\frac{7}{16}$ inches
(77.62 × 57 cm.). Hirshhorn Museum and Sculpture Garden,
Smithsonian Institution, Washington, D.C.

Study and compare
how Marc and Picasso
used rhythm in their
paintings.

▶ What art element do
you see repeated in
each painting?

▶ Look at *Animals in a
Landscape.* Which
element most attracts
your eye: line, shape,
or color? Explain.

▶ Which painting
seems active, and
which seems calm?

Aesthetic Perception

Design Awareness Think about a line of people or a row of books on a
shelf. How do these two rows move? What if there is a break in the line, or a
few of the books lie in a small stack?

Using Rhythm

Rhythm is a principle of design. **Rhythm** organizes the elements of art in a work by repeating elements and objects. In music, rhythm is created by the pause or rest between musical sounds. There is a beat followed by a rest. In a piece of art, visual rhythm is created by repeated positive shapes separated by negative spaces. The shapes are the "beats"; the spaces that separate them are the "rests." Visual rhythm pulls the viewer's eyes through a work of art.

Visual rhythm can be found in nature and in objects made by people.

Practice

Act out visual rhythm in a group.

1. Form a group of four to five people. Within the group, plan two or three ways to arrange the people to create visual rhythm.

2. Present your visual rhythm to the class. See if they can clap the beat and rest between the forms (the people).

3. Take turns with other groups performing your visual rhythms.

◀ **John Gaston.**
Age 11.

Think about how this student artist created rhythm in the design.

 Creative Expression

Create rhythm using lines and shapes in a nonobjective design.

1. Select a shape and a line. Repeat parallel lines and shapes to create visual rhythm. Place them so that your entire paper is covered. Make your design nonobjective; there should be no recognizable objects in your composition.

2. Once your design is drawn to your satisfaction, use a felt-tip marker to trace over your lines.

3. Look at the color schemes in Unit 2. Select one color scheme to use in your nonobjective design. Use color pencils to add color to complete your design.

Art Criticism

Describe Describe your composition.

Analyze Which color scheme did you use in your design? How did you arrange your art elements to create rhythm?

Interpret Give your nonobjective design a title.

Decide Were you successful in creating a nonobjective design using lines and shapes to create rhythm? Explain.

Visual Movement

▲ **Henri Rousseau.** (French).
Exotic Landscape. 1910.

Oil on canvas. $51\frac{1}{4} \times 64$ inches
(130.18 × 162.56 cm.). Norton
Simon Museum, Pasadena, California.

Look closely at the works of art by Rousseau and Cézanne. Henri Rousseau never lived in the exotic places his paintings depict. Instead, his paintings are based on his imagination and on images from books and personal sketches. He often visited the zoo and botanical garden, studying what he saw and creating detailed drawings. Rousseau was a self-taught artist and began painting after age forty. Paul Cézanne began his career with the impressionist painters in Paris. This group painted outdoors or from photographs. Although *Bottom of the Ravine* is a landscape, it was not painted outside or from a photograph. Instead, Cézanne created his landscape from several images in his sketchbooks, arranging them into one composition. Notice how the painted shapes and colors lead your eyes through both paintings.

Art History and Culture

Do both of the paintings have the same subject matter?

▲ **Paul Cézanne.** (French).
Bottom of the Ravine. 1879.
....
Oil on canvas. $28\frac{3}{4} \times 21\frac{1}{4}$ inches
(73.03 × 53.98 cm.). Museum of
Fine Arts, Houston, Texas.

Study both works of art to see how visual movement is used.

▶ Which elements or objects pull your eyes through each work?

▶ What object or area do you see first in Rousseau's painting? Describe the direction in which your eyes move when you look at *Exotic Landscape.*

▶ What object or area do you notice first in *Bottom of the Ravine?* Describe the direction in which your eyes move when you look at this painting.

▶ Which painting is the most active and which one is the most calm?

Aesthetic Perception

Design Awareness Think about a street in a neighborhood. What are some of the objects that you would see? Are any of these objects repeated?

Using Visual Movement

Have you ever seen an image of repeated circles or curves on the surface of water? When a rock is thrown into a body of calm water, we see a rippling effect. In one ring after another, the circles move from where the rock landed. The photograph captures this effect. You do not see the actual movement: the repeated circles and curved lines cause your eyes to move away from the center. Repeated windows on a building make your eyes move across the building. While driving in a car, have you ever noticed fence or telephone poles? The repeated posts and poles pull your eyes along as you are driving by. These are all examples of movement. **Movement** is the principle of art that leads a viewer's eyes through a work of art.

Artists use **visual movement** in a work of art by repeating art elements or objects. Look at the photographs on this page. Notice how the repeated lines, shapes, colors, and objects lead your eyes through the images.

Practice

As a group, arrange cut shapes to create visual movement.

1. Look through the shapes you have been given by your teacher. Select a piece of paper as a background color. Do not glue any of your arrangements.

2. Make two arrangements. First, arrange all like shapes to create a path across your background color. Randomly add in two or three other shapes.

3. Make up your own design for your second arrangement.

◀ **Soyeon Hwang.**
Age 12.

Think about what art element or object was used to create visual movement in the student artist's work.

Creative Expression

Show visual movement in a fantasy jungle painting.

1. Look over your sketches and select several of your images to transfer onto your drawing paper. Choose at least one animal to include in your composition and lightly draw it in first. As you draw, fill in any open spaces with overlapping plant shapes.

2. Practice mixing a variety of greens and testing them on a scrap piece of paper. Do this with any color you mix before applying it to your painting.

3. Begin painting the objects in your drawing. First outline your shape with a small paintbrush, then fill it in.

4. Create an area of interest by using a lighter color or different shape.

Art Criticism

Describe Describe the objects in your painting.

Analyze List the colors, lines, shapes, and objects you used to create visual movement.

Interpret Does your work convey a particular feeling? Explain.

Decide Do you feel you were successful in creating visual movement in a fantasy jungle painting? Explain.

Kinetic Movement

▲ **Alexander Calder.** (American).
Lobster Trap and Fish Tail. 1939.

Painted steel, wire, and sheet aluminum.
8 feet 6 inches × 9 feet 6 inches (2.6 × 2.9 m.).
Museum of Modern Art, New York, New York.

Look closely at the works of art by Alexander Calder and Timothy Rose. Both works are example of mobiles that hang from a ceiling. Alexander Calder invented the mobile in 1932. He named his works after they were installed in their settings. His last mobile, *Untitled,* was installed in the National Gallery of Art in Washington, D.C. after his death. You can see some similarities when you look at *Lobster Trap and Fish Tail* and *Double Pan Swoosh.* These mobiles contain painted cutout shapes connected by wires. Air currents set them in motion. Watching these mobiles move is like watching graceful dancers.

Art History and Culture

Do you think Alexander Calder's mobiles influenced the work of Timothy Rose?

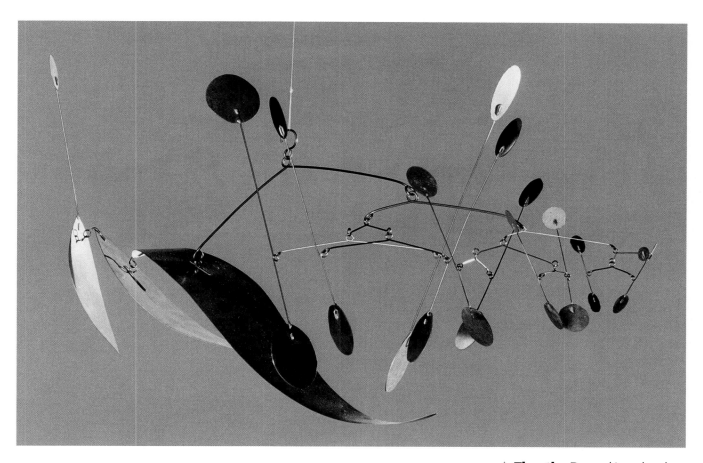

Study both works of art to see how kinetic movement is used.

▶ Which elements or objects do you see repeated in each artwork?

▶ Which lines or shapes appear to move in *Lobster Trap and Fish Tail*?

▶ Which lines or shapes appear to move in *Double Pan Swoosh*?

▶ Describe how you think both mobiles move.

🔍 Aesthetic Perception

Design Awareness Think about banners or flags you have seen outdoors. What do they look like when they are hanging? What effect does a soft breeze have on them?

Using Kinetic Movement

Kinetic movement is actual or real movement. Artists can sometimes control the way their sculpture moves by limiting the amount of motion. A pendulum on a clock swings back and forth and only at a controlled distance. In other sculptural forms, such as a mobile, movement is unpredictable. The wind or air currents may move the objects on a mobile slightly or not at all.

It is difficult to capture kinetic movement in a painting or drawing. A group of artists known as the "futurists" portrayed the idea of movement in their paintings. They used overlapping and slanting lines and shapes to make painted surfaces seem as if they were moving. Alexander Calder believed in what the futurists were doing. In his work he repeated shapes, but unlike the futurists, his shapes really moved. He used the natural forces of gravity and air currents to put his sculptures into real motion. Calder's creation of the mobile is called a "kinetic sculpture" because it actually moves in space.

Practice

Experiment with kinetic movement.

1. Cut four equal-sized shapes of paper.

2. Punch a hole at the top and bottom of each shape.

3. Use paper clips to connect the shapes together. Try different configurations.

◄ **Courtney Davis.**
Age 11.

Think about what shapes or objects the student artist used in the mobile.

Creative Expression

Create a graceful moving mobile using wire and mat board.

1. Look over your list in the Ideas section of your Art Journal. Select one subject and begin by sketching simple shapes or objects.

2. Select five or seven of your images to transfer onto your pieces of mat board. Punch a hole in the top of each shape. Use sandpaper to smooth out the cut edges of your board by sanding in one direction.

3. Use acrylic paints to paint your shapes.

4. Lay out your shapes on a large piece of newspaper. Draw the wire lines showing how the pieces will connect. Begin at the bottom and work your way up.

5. Follow the Mobile Technique Tip, and connect your mobile. Attach the top bar last.

Art Criticism

Describe Describe the subject of your mobile.

Analyze List the colors, lines, shapes, and objects you used to create your mobile.

Interpret Does your mobile communicate your subject matter? Explain.

Decide Do you feel you were successful in creating a mobile using kinetic movement? Explain.

Rhythm, Movement, and Pattern

▲ **Wayne Thiebaud.** (American).
Down Eighteenth Street. 1980.

Oil and charcoal on canvas. 48 × 35$\frac{7}{8}$ inches (121.92 × 91.14 cm.). The Hirshhorn
Museum and Sculpture Garden, Smithsonian Institution, Washington, D.C.

Art Criticism   Critical Thinking

Describe **What do you see?**

During this step you will collect information about the subject of the work.

▶ List all of the things you see.

▶ Describe how the environment changes from the foreground to the background.

Analyze **How is this work organized?**

Think about how the artist has used the elements and principles of art.

▶ What types of lines do you see?

▶ What is the main color scheme?

▶ Where do you see patterns?

▶ Where do you see rhythmic repetition?

▶ How does the artist create visual movement?

Interpret **What does the artwork say?**

Combine clues you collected during description and analysis with your personal experiences to find out what this painting is about.

▶ What season and what time of day does this work express?

▶ How does the artist's use of elements and principles affect the expressive quality of this work?

▶ Has the artist made this a place you would like to visit? Why or why not?

Decide **What do you think about the work?**

Use all the information you have gathered to decide why this is a successful work of art.

▶ Is this work successful because it is realistic? Because it is well organized? Because it conveys a message? Explain.

Show What You Know

Answer these questions on a separate sheet of paper.

1 In a piece of art, _____ is created by repeated positive shapes separated by negative spaces.
  A. texture
  B. visual rhythm
  C. color scheme

2 A _____ is a repeated surface decoration.
  A. motif
  B. space
  C. pattern

3 _____ movement is actual or real movement.
  A. Visual
  B. Kinetic
  C. Active

4 _____ is the principle of art that leads a viewer's eyes through a work of art.
  A. Pattern
  B. Rhythm
  C. Movement

5 A _____ pattern occurs when the motif is repeated in no apparent order.
  A. random
  B. alternating
  C. regular

CAREERS IN ART
Art Historian

People who study art history have many career options. They can work for organizations and businesses, but many art historians choose to work in museums.

Archivists determine what portion of the records maintained by various groups should be made part of permanent historical holdings and which of these records should be put on exhibit.

Curators oversee collections in museums and historic sites. They also plan and prepare exhibits. Most curators use computer databases to catalogue and organize their collections.

Conservators document, treat, and preserve works of art. They examine objects and determine their condition. They then document their findings and treat items to minimize deterioration or restore them to their original state.

▲ **Conservator**

Pattern, Rhythm, and Movement in Dance

▲ African American Dance Ensemble. "Isicathulo."

Isicathulo is a Zulu step dance from South Africa. Zulu dock workers and gold miners perform clever, syncopated routines accompanied by a guitar and whistle. They create rhythmic dances by organizing their well-rehearsed patterns of movements. They discovered that they could make great sounds by slapping and clicking their rubber boots together.

What to Do Make rhythmic patterns of sounds that can be organized different ways to create dances.

Work in small groups to create three or four rhythmic patterns that can be repeated. Give each pattern or routine a name. Choose one of the following or create your own: "bicycle," "salute," or "jump." Following each other or shoulder to shoulder, each rhythmic pattern must be well rehearsed and performed in unison. Dancers do a stamping walk in place until the leader calls out the name of a pattern, which they perform together.

1. Create a rhythmic movement that can be repeated. Include slapping your legs, stamping, clicking fingers, clapping, jumping, or hopping. Give your pattern a name.

2. Get into groups of three or four. Each person shares one pattern and teaches it to the others.

3. Practice all of the patterns in a line formation and perform in unison.

4. Choose a leader to call out the name of each pattern to be performed.

 **Art Criticism**

Describe What patterns did your group learn?

Analyze Does the name of each pattern provide a clue for the movement?

Interpret Did the rhythmic patterns "feel" right? Did you change them to work better?

Decide Were you successful in making the rhythm and movements work together?

Balance and Emphasis

◀ **Rembrandt van Rijn.** (Dutch).
Portrait of Rembrandt. 1650.
Oil on canvas. $36\frac{1}{4} \times 29\frac{3}{4}$ inches (92.08 × 75.57 cm.).
National Gallery of Art, Washington, D.C.

Artists use balance and emphasis to arrange the art elements in a variety of artwork.

The Dutch artist Rembrandt van Rijn is best known for his portraits and paintings of everyday events. He used a technique called *chiaroscuro,* or bright light against a dark area, in his paintings. His ability to paint anything made him one of the most popular artists of his time.

Self-portrait

Artists use different types of balance in all types of artwork.

▶ What objects do you see?

▶ Pretend there is an imaginary line down the center of the painting. Describe how each half is arranged.

Artists can make the viewer look at certain areas in an artwork by using emphasis.

▶ What art element does Rembrandt van Rijn use to make you look at his self-portrait?

▶ Look at the painting. Close your eyes and then open them. What is the first area you see in this painting?

In This Unit you will learn how artists use balance. You will create personal works of art using a variety of media based on formal, informal, and radial balance. You also will learn about emphasis of an art element and how to emphasize an area.

Here are the topics you will study:
▶ Formal balance
▶ Symmetry
▶ Approximate symmetry
▶ Informal balance
▶ Asymmetry
▶ Radial balance
▶ Emphasis
▶ Focal point

Rembrandt van Rijn
(1606–1669)

Rembrandt was born in Leiden, in the Netherlands. He was the youngest of ten children and was given the opportunity to study art at a young age. He began teaching drawing and painting at the age of twenty-two. He is often referred to as the greatest Dutch painter of his era. Rembrandt painted portraits, everyday events, historical subjects, and landscapes. Wealthy citizens of Amsterdam were pleased with his style because he could paint the fine details of their clothing without detracting from the subject. Rembrandt was also skilled in the technique of chiaroscuro, which resulted in powerful and impressive portraits. It is believed he painted between fifty and sixty self-portraits.

Formal Balance and Symmetry

▲ **United States Capitol.**
1793–1830; 1851–1863.
....
Stone-bearing masonry and cast-iron
dome. Washington, D.C.

Look at the architectural structures on these two pages. The United States Capitol is one of the most important buildings in the world. It was originally built in three sections, under the supervision of six different architects and United States presidents. Over the course of two centuries, it has endured a fire and been rebuilt, extended, and restored. The Eiffel Tower of Paris was designed by French engineer Alexandre-Gustave Eiffel. He designed the tower for the 1889 world's fair; it was intended to last for only twenty years. It is an early example of large-scale, wrought-iron construction. The lower level has a restaurant, and elevators and a stairway take visitors to the top of the tower.

Art History and Culture

What other historic landmarks are located in Washington, D.C., and in Paris, France?

Study how formal balance is used by looking closely at both architectural structures.

▶ Describe how the shapes are arranged in the *United States Capitol*.

▶ How are lines and shapes repeated and arranged in the *Eiffel Tower?*

▶ Imagine a line drawn down the center of each structure. Describe what you see on either side of the center line.

▶ Think about the type of feeling you get when you look at each of these structures. Is it calm or uneasy? Explain.

▲ **Alexandre-Gustave Eiffel.** (French).
Eiffel Tower. 1887–1889.
Exposed iron. 985 feet high (300.23 meters). Paris, France.

Aesthetic Perception

Design Awareness We are surrounded by architectural structures in our community that are available to everyone. Think about a public structure that is identical on each side.

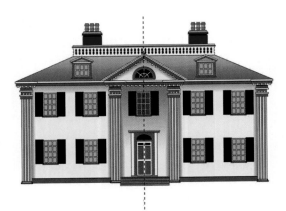

Using Formal Balance and Symmetry

Look around you. You are looking at examples of balance and may not even be aware of it. Examine your chair, a table, and your clothes; consider your walk—all of these are balanced. We live with balance daily. A work of art must contain balance. **Balance** is the principle of design that relates to visual weight in an artwork. Visual balance causes the viewer to feel that the elements have been arranged just right. Artists often balance the art elements along an imaginary dividing line. This imaginary line is called the **central axis.** The central axis can run in two directions: vertically and horizontally.

Formal balance is one type of balance. **Formal balance** occurs when equal or similar elements are placed on opposite sides of a central axis. The central axis can be imaginary or real. **Symmetry** is a type of formal balance in which two halves of a balanced artwork are mirror images of each other. Symmetry gives the feeling of dignity, endurance, and stability. Furniture and clothing are usually symmetrical. Too much symmetry, however, can be dull because it is so predictable.

Notice the location of the central axes of these two symmetrical images.

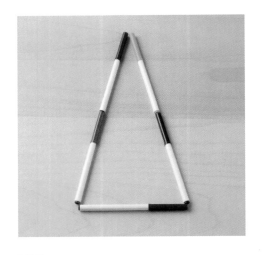

Practice

Arrange five similar objects to show formal balance.

1. Look around your classroom for objects that are similar in size and shape, such as markers, pencils, paper clips, or crayons.

2. At your table and with a group, arrange the five items in a way that shows formal balance.

3. See how many different arrangements you can make. Discuss the differences and similarities that you notice.

◄ **Allison Keeling.**
Age 11.

Think about how the student artist used symmetrical balance in this public-building design.

Creative Expression

Use symmetrical balance to design a public building.

1. Use one of the ideas in your Art Journal to create two sketches. Use basic shapes and architectural elements. Look at the architectural details that you collected in your Art Journal for ideas.

2. Look over your two sketches and decide which one you like best. Lightly transfer your sketch onto drawing paper. Use a ruler to help you draw straight lines.

3. Add architectural textures such as wood or stone to make your design more interesting. Decide where your building will be located and add a background.

4. After your drawing is complete, outline it using a fine-tip black marker. Use watercolor paints to complete your design.

Art Criticism

Describe Describe your public building.

Analyze Describe how you created symmetrical balance in your design.

Interpret What details did you use to communicate the type of public building you designed?

Decide Do you feel you successfully designed a public building using symmetrical balance? Explain.

Lesson 2
Approximate Symmetry

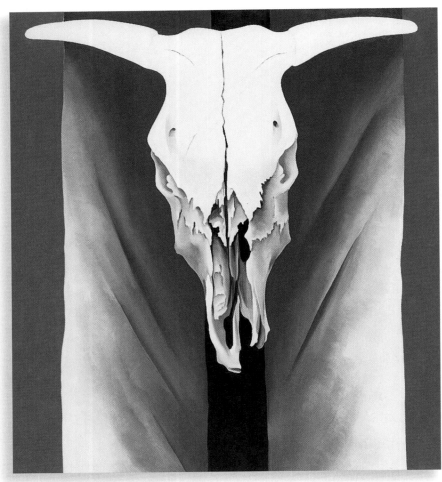

Look closely at the two paintings on these pages. Both works of art show a head-on view of the subject matter. In *Cow's Skull: Red White and Blue*, Georgia O'Keeffe placed the skull almost in the center of the painting. She is best known for her close-up views of flowers and animal bones. Most of her famous images were painted in New Mexico. Ferdinand Hodler painted *James Vibert, Sculptor* so large that the subject's shoulders barely fit within the canvas frame. Vilbert was a friend of Hodler's. In both paintings, the two sides are almost mirror images of each other. Both paintings illustrate approximate symmetry.

▲ **Georgia O'Keeffe.** (American).
Cow's Skull: Red White and Blue. 1931.

Oil on canvas. $39\frac{7}{8} \times 37\frac{7}{8}$ inches (101.3 × 96.22 cm.).
Metropolitan Museum of Art, New York, New York.

Art History and Culture

What other paintings have you studied that look symmetrical but really are not?

▲ **Ferdinand Hodler.**
(Swiss). *James Vibert, Sculptor.* 1907.

Oil on canvas. $25\frac{3}{4} \times 26\frac{1}{8}$ inches
(65.41 × 66.35 cm.). Art Institute
of Chicago, Chicago, Illinois.

Study how approximate symmetry is used in the paintings by O'Keeffe and Hodler.

▶ Describe where the objects are placed in the compositions.

▶ Look at Hodler's painting. Why does it not show perfect symmetry?

▶ Imagine a line drawn down the center of *Cow's Skull: Red White and Blue.* Describe what happens on each side of the central axis.

▶ Think about the type of feeling you get when you look at each of these paintings. How does this type of balance affect those feelings?

Aesthetic Perception

Seeing Like an Artist Can you think of any objects in nature that are almost, but not quite, identical on both sides?

Using Approximate Symmetry

Sometimes artists choose a balance for an artwork based on a feeling it expresses. Formal balance can sometimes be too stiff and formal, so artists will use another type of formal balance called *approximate symmetry* that has a calm feeling. **Approximate symmetry** is a type of balance that is almost symmetrical, but small differences in the artwork make it more interesting.

To avoid boring the viewer, artists often use approximate symmetry. Like symmetry, it is stable, but small differences make the arrangement more interesting. Your face is an example of approximate symmetry. If you look in a mirror you will notice that the two halves of your face are not exactly identical.

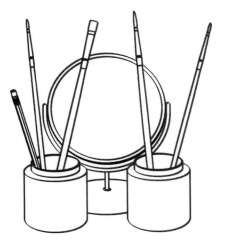

Notice how approximate symmetry can be found in nature and in objects made by people.

Practice

Draw a common object to show approximate symmetry.

1. Look around your classroom for objects that are almost symmetrical.

2. Create a line drawing showing the shape of your selected item. Look closely at the details.

3. Arrange your composition so that your object is large and is almost in the center. Save your drawing. What about the object makes it an example of approximate symmetry?

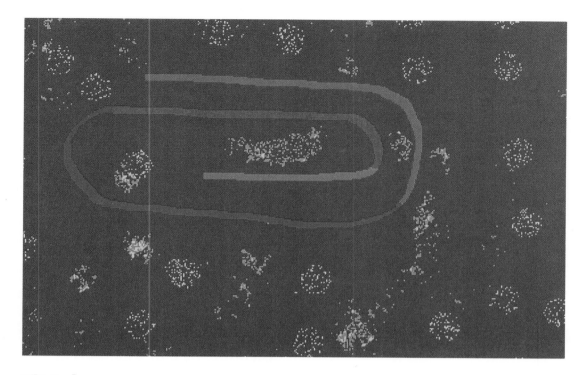

◀ **Sam Sheffield.**
Age 12.

Think about how this student artist used approximate symmetry in the design.

 **Creative Expression**

Use approximate symmetry to create a computer-generated design.

1. Look at your collected images in your Art Journal. Choose one or two images.

2. Use a computer draw or paint program and the mouse to draw your interpretation of the selected images. Do not include anything from the images' background.

3. Create a copy of your images and save them. Use a variety of tools on the menu to create a design using approximate symmetry.

4. After your drawing is complete, select either a warm or cool color for your background. Create interest by using a contrasting color to complete your design. Title and save your work.

Art Criticism

Describe What object(s) did you select to use?

Analyze Describe how you created approximate symmetry in your design.

Interpret How does your selected color scheme affect the mood of your artwork? Is it calm or active?

Decide Do you think you were successful in creating a computer-generated design using approximate symmetry? Explain.

Informal Balance

Look closely at the two works of art on these pages. Katsushika Hokusai was raised by a family of craftsmen who taught him how to engrave the back of mirrors. He later applied what he had learned to carving woodblocks and became a successful printmaker. Mary Cassatt was the only American artist to join the French impressionists. She created many paintings like *The Tea,* in which she captured a moment of everyday life. The impressionists were influenced by photography and Japanese prints. Both of these mediums allowed artists to crop the image and capture the moment. Look at *The Tea.* Notice how a portion of the fireplace is off the canvas. This technique is called *cropping.* Notice the arrangement of the objects in both of these works.

◀ **Katsushika Hokusai.** (Japanese).
Li Bai. 1834.
Woodblock print. $20\frac{1}{2} \times 9\frac{1}{8}$ inches (52.1 × 23.2 cm.).
Honolulu Academy of Arts, Honolulu, Hawaii.

 Art History and Culture

Look at the dates and titles of these works of art. What kinds of people are depicted by these artists?

▲ **Mary Cassatt.** (American). *The Tea.* 1879.

Oil on canvas. $25\frac{1}{2} \times 36\frac{1}{2}$ inches (64.77 × 92.71 cm.). Museum of Fine Arts, Boston, Massachusetts.

Study both works of art to better understand informal balance.

▶ List the objects in both works of art.

▶ How are the objects arranged in *The Tea?*

▶ Which are the largest objects in both works of art? Where are they placed?

▶ Imagine a line drawn down the center of each work of art. Describe what happens on either side of the center line.

Aesthetic Perception

Design Awareness Think about photographs you have seen. How are the people usually arranged? Are they always in the center of the photograph or to one side?

Using Informal Balance

Think about riding in a car. A road divides your view in half and is symmetrically balanced. The objects on either side are probably not the same, but they take up the same amount of space. **Informal balance** is a way of organizing parts of a design so that unlike objects have equal visual weight. *Asymmetry* is another name for informal balance. The negative space, or the areas around the object or group of objects, is often larger on one side of an asymmetrical piece than on the other side. Artists create asymmetrical balance in several ways.

Size: A large shape or form appears to be heavier than a small shape. Several small shapes can balance one large shape. To create informal balance, artists place large shapes closer to the center and small shapes farther away.

Color: A bright color has more visual weight than a dull color.

Texture: A rough texture has an uneven pattern of highlights and shadows. For this reason, a rough surface attracts the viewer's eyes more easily than a smooth, even surface.

Position: A larger, positive shape and a small, negative space can be balanced by a small, positive shape and a large, negative space.

Practice

Collect images that have asymmetrical balance from a magazine.

1. Find three examples of asymmetrical balance based on size, color, texture, or position.

2. Cut out the images and fold them in half. Using a marker, outline the objects on each side of the folded line.

3. Notice how the objects are arranged, and discuss this with your table group. Glue your collected images onto a piece of paper. Below each image, list how balance was achieved by size, color, texture, or position. Place this in your Art Journal.

◄ **Sussy Pelaez.**
Age 11.

Think about how this student artist used asymmetrical balance in the still-life drawing.

 **Creative Expression**

Use asymmetrical balance to create a still-life drawing using color chalk.

1. Arrange a variety of objects to create a still life. Include tall and short objects, and items with various patterns and colors.

2. Create two quick sketches from different viewpoints using asymmetrical balance. Select the one you like best.

3. Use white chalk to transfer your sketch onto black paper. Use white glue to outline your drawing. Let it dry.

4. Use color chalk to add color to your still-life drawing.

5. Give your completed work a title.

Art Criticism

Describe Describe the objects in your still life.

Analyze How did you create asymmetrical balance in your still life?

Interpret How did your choice of colors affect the mood of your still life?

Decide Do you feel you successfully created a color-chalk still life using asymmetrical balance? Explain.

Radial Balance

◄ **Attributed to Alverda Herb.** (American). *Bull's Eye Quilt.* c. 1900–1920.

Cotton. $84\frac{1}{2} \times 86$ inches (214.63 × 218.44 cm.). American Folk Art Museum, New York, New York.

Look at the works of art on these two pages. Do you see the designs radiating from the center of each artwork? These images are examples of radial balance. *Bull's Eye Quilt* is attributed to Alverda Herb, because evidence suggests that someone in the family made the quilt. However, historians are not completely certain who it was. The akrafokonmu were made by the Asante people, who live along the Gold Coast of West Africa. These discs act as a talisman or amulet, and are worn by individuals who represent the soul of the chief. The discs are found in many places in West Africa and are usually worn around the neck, hanging from a fiber cord or a gold chain.

 Art History and Culture

Would you classify these pieces of art as abstract or utilitarian?

▲ **Artist unknown.**
(Asante). *Akrafokonmu (Soul Discs).* Twentieth century.
• •
Gold. Largest diameter: $4\frac{1}{2}$ inches (11.43 cm.). The Museum of Fine Arts, Houston, Texas.

Study how radial balance is used by looking closely at the works of art.

▶ Describe the shapes and how they are arranged in the works of art.

▶ Look closely at *Akrafokonmu (Soul Discs).* Which area attracts your eye? Why?

▶ Of the designs on these pages, which show the most movement? Why?

▶ Where do the designs begin and end in *Bull's Eye Quilt?*

Aesthetic Perception

Design Awareness Think about other objects you have seen that radiate, or come out, from the center.

Using Radial Balance

Radial balance is a type of balance that occurs when the art elements come out, or radiate, from a central point. Radial balance is a variation of symmetry. Instead of having two matching units, it has four or more. In radial design, the central axis is the center point. Another name for this center point is the focal point. The **focal point** is the area of an artwork that is emphasized.

Radial balance occurs frequently in nature. If you look at a daisy or sunflower, you will notice that the petals radiate outward from the center. People have imitated nature by producing many objects that have radial designs. Spokes on a bicycle and hands on a clock are examples of radial balance.

A radial design created with straight lines radiating from the axis produces a calming effect. If a radial design is swirling outward from the center, it gives a feeling of excitement.

Practice

Fold a paper to create radial balance.

1. Fold a square piece of paper in half. Open the paper. Notice how the two sides are symmetrical. Close the paper.

2. Fold the paper a second time so that it becomes square again. What happens when you open it? Keep the paper open.

3. Create a third and fourth fold so that the corners of the paper touch. Your paper should be divided into eight sections, all radiating outward from the axis.

◀ **Harry Jones.**
Age 11.

Think about what shapes the student artist began with when creating this radial design.

 Creative Expression

Use shapes and a color scheme to create a radial design.

1. Lightly trace a circle on your paper with eight pie shapes.

2. Draw one shape in the center of your radial design for your focal point. Complete your design by using the shapes you made in your Art Journal. Outline your drawing using a fine-tip permanent marker.

3. Select a color scheme using three or more colors that you like. Use color pencils or markers to complete your radial design.

4. Display it for your classmates to see.

 **Art Criticism**

Describe What shape did you use as your focal point?

Analyze What shapes and color scheme did you select for the rest of your design? Why?

Interpret What does your radial design remind you of?

Decide Do you feel you were able to successfully create a radial design using repeated shapes and a color scheme? Explain.

Emphasis of an Element

▲ **Susan Rothenberg.**
(American). *Cabin Fever.*
1976.
....
Acrylic and tempera on canvas.
67 × 84⅛ inches (170.18 × 213.67
cm.). Modern Art Museum of Fort
Worth, Texas.

Look at the two works of art. William Sharp created *Great Water Lily of America* using a technique called *chromolithography*. Like lithography, the image is drawn on a litho stone. However, Sharp used multiple stones, one for each color. Susan Rothenberg is best known for her abstract images of horse silhouettes. She began creating her paintings accidentally. She doodled a rough horse image onto a small sheet of paper and liked what she saw. Both works of art are examples of emphasis through contrast. For instance, in *Cabin Fever,* the shape of the horse dominates the image because it is the only shape. The color red is important, but not as important as the horse's shape.

 Art History and Culture

Examine these works of art. Before looking at the dates, decide which one looks older.

Study both works of art and compare how the artist used emphasis through contrast.

▶ Describe the objects in both works of art.

▶ What object or area do you see first in each work of art? Why?

▶ Where in the painting are the main objects located?

▶ Which painting is active, and which one is calm?

▲ **William Sharp.**
(English/American).
Great Water Lily of America. 1854.

Chromolithograph on woven white paper.
$21\frac{1}{4}$ × 27 inches (53.98 × 68.58 cm.). Amon Carter Museum, Fort Worth, Texas.

Aesthetic Perception

Design Awareness Think about a time when you have seen a line of cars on the expressway or on a busy street. Did any one car stand out more than the others? If so, why?

Using Emphasis of an Element

In advertisements, music, and your day-to-day communications, you see and hear certain ideas and feelings emphasized over others. In art, emphasis is used in the same way.

Emphasis is the principle of design that stresses one area in an artwork over another area. Emphasis of an art element occurs when one art element dominates the entire work, and the other elements become less important.

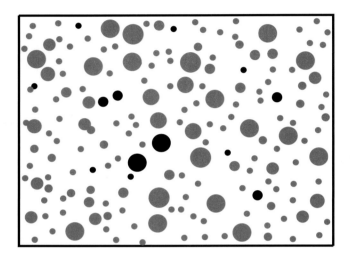

Practice

Cut three shapes and create a crayon rubbing to show emphasis.

1. Cut out your shapes from tagboard. Make two geometric and one free-form shape.

2. Place a shape on the table and place your paper on top of the shape. Rub the top of the paper with the side of a crayon. The outline of the shape below will transfer onto the paper.

3. Experiment with creating a crayon rubbing of each shape, with overlapping shapes, and with using contrasting colors. What happens when you overlap shapes?

◀ **Shawna Sullivan.**
Age 11.

Think about what art element or object the student artist used to create emphasis in this artwork.

Creative Expression

Make a **collograph** print using contrast, isolation, or placement to create emphasis.

1. You will be layering each of your shapes to create a collage of your image. Look at your plant sketch in your Art Journal. Draw and cut out your large shape first. If you are creating a flower, cut out the individual petals and glue these on top of your paper. Glue the center portion last. This is called a printing plate.

2. Once you have glued down all of your shapes, make a crayon rubbing of it. This will allow you to see what your print will look like when it is finished. Make any necessary changes.

3. Set up your printing area, and create a print of your collaged image.

Art Criticism

Describe What plant form did you choose for your print?

Analyze Which art element was emphasized? Which technique did you use?

Interpret Write a poem based on your print.

Decide Do you feel you were successful in creating a collograph print using emphasis? Explain.

Emphasis of Area

▲ **George Segal.**
(American). *Three People on Four Park Benches.* 1979.
. . . .
Plaster and real benches. Life-size. New Orleans Museum of Art, New Orleans, Louisiana.

Look closely at the sculptures by George Segal and Juan Muñoz. Both works are examples of sculpture installations in which the environment becomes part of the artwork. Segal creates sculptures of everyday people in everyday situations. He creates the molds using surgical gauze and plaster. His models pose as he wraps the gauze in sections on their bodies. As each section dries, he cuts the gauze off. He then puts the sections together again using plaster until he has created a whole person. *Conversation Piece* by Juan Muñoz is based on a concept from the Renaissance and was influenced by Segal's work. One or more figures interact with one another to create a lifelike situation. What do you think the groups of people are talking about?

 Art History and Culture

Look at the dates of these sculptures. Do you think the meaning of these works of art have changed over time?

▲ **Juan Muñoz.** (Spanish).
Conversation Piece. 1994–1995.

Bronze. Variable dimensions, each approximately $64\frac{1}{2} \times 204 \times 228$ inches (163.8 × 518.2 × 579.1 cm.). Hirshhorn Museum and Sculpture Garden, Washington, D.C.

Study both sculptures to gain a better understanding of how emphasis of area is used.

▶ Which elements or objects do you see repeated in each artwork?

▶ How did George Segal create the feeling of isolation in *Three People on Four Park Benches?*

▶ How did Juan Muñoz arrange his figures?

▶ Which part of each of these works of art do you notice first?

Aesthetic Perception

Design Awareness Think about a sporting event or dance you have attended. Describe how people interacted with one another.

Using Emphasis of Area

You have learned that **emphasis** is the principle of design that stresses one area in an artwork over another area. Two types of visual emphasis can be used: emphasis of an art element and emphasis of an area. Sometimes a specific area in an artwork is emphasized. This area is called the **focal point.** There are several techniques that artists use to create emphasis.

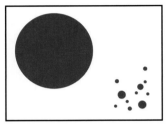
Contrast

Contrast occurs when one element stands out from the rest of the work. A bright color stands out from a dull color. A large shape stands out from small shapes. An angular shape among round shapes catches the viewer's attention. A rough texture against a smooth texture catches the viewer's eye.

Isolation

Isolation occurs when an object is placed alone and away from the other objects in an artwork. The viewer's eye is drawn to the isolated object.

Location

Location occurs when the eyes are naturally drawn toward the center of an artwork. Anything placed near the center of the work will be noticed first.

Practice

Create a focal point in a gesture drawing.

1. Create a series of gesture drawings using crayons. Look at the list you generated in the Idea section of your Art Journal. Take turns posing based on the ideas in your list.

2. Make drawings quickly with few or no details.

3. Create several of your gesture drawings, using one or two colors. At some point, create one of your gestures in a third color. Try to fit as many gestures as you can onto your paper.

◀ **Michelle Leonard's sixth-grade class.**

Think about how the students created an area of emphasis in their group sculpture.

 **Creative Expression**

Create an individual foil sculpture to be displayed together with other foil sculptures to emphasize an area.

1. Review your list of locations in your Art Journal. As a class, select one location. Look over your Practice gesture drawings and select one, or create a new one.

2. Create a wire figure based on your selected gesture. The wire figure is an **armature,** the framework for supporting the foil that will be used for your sculpture.

3. Using pieces of aluminum foil no larger than your hand, cover the wire sculpture. You can pinch out a nose or add clothing with more foil.

4. Attach your completed foil sculpture to a base, if necessary. As a class, arrange your sculptures for display.

Art Criticism

Describe Describe the location of your group sculpture.

Analyze How did you create an area of emphasis?

Interpret Does your group sculpture communicate the idea you selected? Explain.

Decide Were you successful in creating your individual sculpture? As a group, were you able to create an area of emphasis? Explain.

Balance and Emphasis

◀ **Alice Neel.** (American). *Loneliness.* 1970.
. . . .
Oil on canvas. 80 × 38 inches (203.2 × 96.52 cm.).
National Gallery of Art, Washington, D.C.

Art Criticism | Critical Thinking

Describe **What do you see?**

During this step you will collect information about the subject of the artwork.

► List all of the things you see in the foreground.

► List all of the objects you see in the middle ground.

► List all of the things you see in the background.

Analyze **How is this work organized?**

Think about how the artist used the elements and principles of art.

► What colors or color scheme dominates the painting?

► What type of balance was used to place the chair?

► What object do you see first? What makes it stand out? What object do you see next?

Interpret **What does the artwork say?**

Combine clues you collected during Describe and Analyze with your personal experiences to find out what this painting is about.

► What time of day is it?

► What type of building do you think this room is in? Why?

► Who do you think sits in the chair?

► Why do you think Alice Neel titled this work *Loneliness?*

Decide **What do you think about the work?**

Use all the information you have gathered to decide why this is a successful work of art.

► Is this work of art successful because it is realistic, because it is well organized, or because it conveys a message?

Balance and Emphasis, continued

Show What You Know

Answer these questions on a separate sheet of paper.

1 _____ is a type of balance that is almost symmetrical, but small differences in the artwork make it more interesting.
A. Average symmetry
B. Approximate symmetry
C. Appropriate symmetry

2 _____ is the principle of design that relates to visual weight in an artwork.
A. Color
B. Emphasis
C. Balance

3 _____ is the principle of design that stresses one area in an artwork over another area.
A. Emphasis
B. Line
C. Balance

4 _____ is a type of formal balance in which two halves of a balanced artwork are identical, mirror images of each other.
A. Asymmetry
B. Radial balance
C. Symmetry

5 The _____ is the area of an artwork that is emphasized.
A. center
B. focal point
C. frame

VISIT A MUSEUM
Norton Simon Museum

The Norton Simon Museum is located in Pasadena, California. It was originally founded in 1924 as the Pasadena Art Institute and reorganized by Norton Simon in 1974. The museum consists of 38 galleries and a sculpture garden. The permanent collection contains Western and Asian art that spans a 2,000-year period. The museum owns works of art by Renaissance artists, such as Raphael and Boticelli, and impressionists, including Monet and Renoir. Pieces created by Picasso, van Gogh, and Matisse also can be found there, as well as works of art by other master artists. The public can visit the museum and view 1,000 works of art on a regular basis. The museum also has rotating special exhibits, so it can present different parts of the permanent collection.

Balance in Dance

The Pilobolus Dance Theatre works with weight and balance to create sculptural dance forms. Each dance starts with "creative play," when the dancers are directed to find new ways of moving and supporting each other's weight. During this improvisation time, there are no rules, just experimentation to find new ideas. These dancers are known for their daring body sculptures, lifts, and balances. Using their knowledge of scientific physics principles, they create inventive body designs and motion. They develop great trust in each other as they work in partnerships to find a center of gravity and balance, to use moving or kinetic energy, and to explore weight, mass, and force.

What to Do With a partner, create sculptural studies that use balance and counterbalance.

1. Work with a partner to explore the following:

   ▶ Face each other and firmly hold wrists. Tuck your hips forward, lean with shoulders back, and bend your knees. Find the balance between you. When you are balanced, keep leaning away and slowly lower your level.

   ▶ Now explore ways to balance, holding only right or left hands in a diagonal hold. When you have found your center of gravity, try lifting a leg.

   ▶ Back to back, press against each other to find balance. Try lowering yourselves while maintaining balance. Experiment by pressing against shoulders or hands.

2. Perform your two best ideas for others in the class.

▲ Pilobolus Dance Theatre. "The Brass Ring" excerpt.

Art Criticism

Describe Describe the scientific principles of "opposing forces."

Analyze What choices did you make in finding pulling or pressing designs?

Interpret What feelings did you have as you tried to find the balance, and when you actually found the balance point?

Decide Did your sculptural studies have symmetry or approximate symmetry?

Proportion, Distortion, and Scale

▲ **Frida Kahlo.** (Mexican).
Frida y Diego Rivera. 1931.
Oil on canvas. 39⅜ × 31 inches (100.01 × 78.74 cm.).
San Francisco Museum of Modern Art, San Francisco, California.

Artists use proportion, distortion, and scale in both sculptural forms and pictures.

Mexican artist Frida Kahlo is best known for her series of self-portraits depicting her life. She used color and objects symbolically to communicate her feelings and experiences. She also used the ongoing theme of pain in her paintings as a result of the hardships she endured during her short life.

Artists use **proportion** to portray human size in two- and three-dimensional works of art.

▶ What objects do you see?

▶ Use your fingers to measure the size of the woman's head. About how many heads tall is she? Measure the man in the same way.

Distortion is used by artists to express feelings and ideas in works of art.

▶ What feeling was Kahlo trying to communicate in her wedding portrait?

▶ Which objects, if any, are larger or smaller than normal?

Scale is used by artists to show the size of one object in relation to another object.

▶ How big are the people in the painting? What gives you a clue about their size?

In This Unit you will learn how artists use proportion. Using a variety of media, you will create personal artwork based on proportion, distortion, and exaggeration. You also will learn about scale as an art principle and how it relates to size. Here are the topics you will study:
▶ Proportion
▶ Ratio
▶ Distortion
▶ Exaggeration
▶ Scale
▶ Surrealism

Frida Kahlo
(1907–1954)

Frida Kahlo was born in Mexico City. As a child she had polio, which caused one leg to grow smaller than the other. During her teens, Kahlo was in a bus accident, which left her severely injured. She endured thirty-five surgical operations and a life of pain. It was while in the hospital that Kahlo taught herself to paint, out of boredom. Later, she became reacquainted with and married muralist Diego Rivera, whom she had met when he was painting a mural in her high school. Many of her paintings are based on her marriage, her pain, and the history of the Mexican people.

Facial Proportions

▲ **Isabel Bishop.** (American).
Two Girls. 1935.
....
Oil and tempera on masonite.
20 × 24 inches (50.8 × 60.96 cm.).
The Metropolitan Museum of Art,
New York, New York.

Look at the paintings by Isabel Bishop and John Singleton Copley. Bishop traveled daily from her home in Riverdale, New York, to her studio in Union Square, Manhattan. During her long daily commute, she sketched. Her subject matter was the working girls she saw as she rode the train. The blonde woman in *Two Girls* is a waitress from the cafe where Bishop ate breakfast. The woman whose face we see was the waitress's friend. Copley was a self-taught artist and was the first American artist to be recognized for his work both in the United States and in Europe. *Henry Pelham* is a painting of Copley's half-brother. This painting was for an exhibition in London to see how the leading artists of England would rate Copley's work. *Henry Pelham* is one of Copley's earliest paintings and is considered one of his finest works.

Art History and Culture

Study the clothes the people are wearing. Do you think they fit the period in which the paintings were created?

◀ **John Singleton Copley.** (American). *Henry Pelham (Boy with a Squirrel).* 1765.

Oil on canvas. 30¼ × 25 inches (76.84 × 63.5 cm.). Museum of Fine Arts, Boston, Massachusetts.

Study the two paintings to better understand facial proportions.

▶ Describe the positions of the faces in the two paintings.

▶ What are the differences in the way the eyes are portrayed? How do the mouths look different?

▶ Where are the ears in relation to the eyes and nose?

▶ Describe where the hairline is in relation to the top of the head in Copley's painting.

Aesthetic Perception

Design Awareness Look at the faces around you. Notice how everyone's features are arranged similarly.

Using Facial Proportions

The principle of art concerned with the size relationship of one part to another is called **proportion.** In realistic portraits, artists use correct proportions. They use facial proportions to help place features correctly on the human face. **Facial proportions** are the relationship of one feature of a face to other features.

Frontal proportions A front view of the head can be divided by drawing three horizontal lines across a vertical center line called the **central axis.** In the example, notice how the eyes are drawn on the center line, the lips just below the bottom line, and the ears between the center and lower horizontal lines. The nose is above the bottom line on the central axis. The hairline is near the top line.

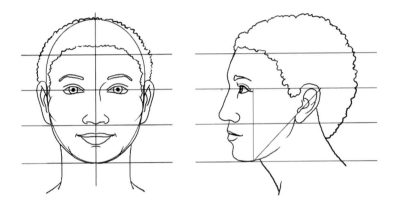

Profile Proportions When you view a head in profile, or from a side view, all the horizontal proportion lines remain the same as in the front view. However, the shape of the head and the shapes of the features change. In the example, notice that the shape of the head in the profile is different from that of the front view. Notice the spaces between the eye, the ear, and the chin.

Practice

Using a marker, make a blind contour drawing.

1. Select a partner, and take turns drawing a blind contour.

2. Look closely at your partner. Place the marker tip on the paper and slowly move the pen as your eyes follow the contours of your partner's face.

3. Try not to pick up the pen or look down at your paper when you draw your partner's profile. See if you can draw your partner's profile in proportion.

◄ **Jonathan Lizcano.**
Age 12.

Think about how the student artist used facial proportions.

 Creative Expression

Use oil pastels to create a self-portrait using facial proportions.

1. Choose one of the sketches from your Art Journal. Begin by using chalk to draw in your facial proportions. Add your features, hair, and clothing to fill the page.

2. Select a color scheme that you think best reflects your personality.

3. Practice blending colors on a scrap piece of paper. Do this by overlapping colors and working them with your oil pastels. Try using a paper towel to blend colors.

4. Use oil pastels to complete your self-portrait.

 **Art Criticism**

Describe List the steps you took in creating your self-portrait.

Analyze Describe how you used a central axis and guide lines to create facial proportions. What color scheme did you use?

Interpret How does your color scheme affect the mood of your self-portrait?

Decide Were you able to use facial proportions successfully in your portrait? Explain.

Figure Proportions

Look at the works of art on these pages. *Armor of George Clifford, Third Earl of Cumberland,* was made for a man who stands five feet nine and a half inches tall. By today's standard this would be considered smaller than average. The marble sculpture *Dancing Lady* was carved around 50 B.C. During this time in ancient Greece it was believed that the human body was the true expression of order. Statues, like *Dancing Lady,* were not realistic portraits, but rather the perfect, or ideal, form. This is why many Greek sculptures from this time period, the Golden Age, look so much alike.

◀ **Royal Workshops.** (England). *Armor of George Clifford, Third Earl of Cumberland.* c. 1580–1585.
••
Steel, etched, blued, and gilded. 69½ inches tall (176.53 cm.). The Metropolitan Museum of Art, New York, New York.

 Art History and Culture

Look at the condition of these works of art. Why do you think they belong in a museum?

Study the armor and the statue to learn about figure proportions.

▶ Use your fingers to measure the length of the head on both works of art. How many heads tall is each piece?

▶ Look at both works of art and describe the similarities.

▶ How tall do you think the statue *Dancing Lady* is? Now look at the size of the image listed in the caption. Explain why you guessed the size that you did.

▶ What did the artist do to make *Dancing Lady* look realistic in size?

◀ **Artist unknown.** (Greece).
Dancing Lady. c. 50 B.C.
....
Marble. 33⅝ inches tall including base
(85.4 cm.). The Cleveland Museum of
Art, Cleveland, Ohio.

Aesthetic Perception

Design Awareness Think about shopping for clothes. How are the clothes usually arranged? Think about the range of sizes and lengths.

Using Figure Proportions

Look around and you will notice that people come in all different shapes and sizes. Still, most people's bodies have similar proportions.

You learned in the previous lesson that **proportion** is the principle of art concerned with the size relationship of one part to another. For example, someone who is six feet tall may have the same proportions as someone who is five feet tall. This means that the taller person's limbs have the same ratio as the shorter person's limbs. A **ratio** is a comparison of size between two things. Artists often use the head as the ratio of *one* to the length of an adult body, which is about seven and a half head lengths. Therefore, the ratio is written as 1:7.5, which means the ratio is 1 (the head) to 7.5 (heads per body length).

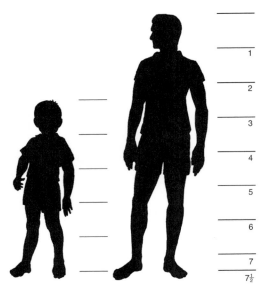

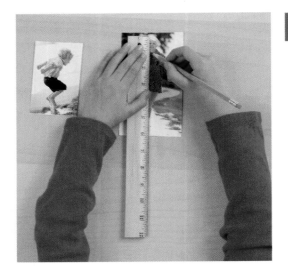

Practice

Compare body proportions.

1. Look through a magazine and cut out a picture of an adult and a child. Make sure that the picture you find is a complete image of the adult and child standing or walking.

2. Measure the head of each person. Use that measurement to see how many head lengths the body is.

3. Compare the ratio of the adult with the ratio of the child. As a class, discuss your findings. Use questions and observations from your Art Journal as part of the discussion if possible.

Think about how the student artist used body proportions in this line drawing.

🎨 Creative Expression

Create a series of line drawings using body proportions.

1. Take turns with your partner posing for one another and making several sketches. Use the sighting technique. Think about body proportions as you create your sketches.

2. Select the sketch you like best and transfer it to drawing paper. Add a prop to your drawing that looks like it belongs, such as a tennis racket. Use a combination of simple thick and thin lines, and draw your image large so that your figure fills the page. Include a background in your drawing.

3. Use a marker to outline your drawing and to add textures. Use hatching, cross-hatching, or stippling techniques to create value.

💬 Art Criticism

Describe Describe the pose you chose. What props did you add?

Analyze How did you use the sighting technique? What techniques did you use to add value?

Interpret What type of mood does your selected pose communicate?

Decide Were you able to use body proportions successfully in your drawing? Explain.

Facial Distortion

▲ **Edvard Munch.** (Norwegian).
The Scream. 1893.
....
Tempera and casein on cardboard. 36 × 29 inches
(91.44 × 73.66 cm.). Munch-Museet, Oslo, Norway.

Look closely at the artwork on these two pages. When it was first exhibited, *The Scream,* by Edvard Munch, shocked viewers because it communicates the emotion of fear. During this time period, paintings usually conveyed happy emotions and were painted with bright colors. *Face Jugs,* from Georgia and South Carolina, are examples of Southern folk pottery. They were first made in the 1800s by the African American potters of the Edgefield District of South Carolina. No one really knows their purpose. The techniques of these early potters filtered into Georgia and eventually throughout the United States.

 Art History and Culture

Examine these works of art. Do they remind you of any other pieces you have studied?

Study the faces portrayed on these two pages to learn more about facial distortion.

▶ What normal human features have been changed in *The Scream?* How have they been altered?

▶ What features look larger than normal in *Face Jugs?* Are any of the features smaller than normal? Explain.

▶ What emotions do you think Munch was communicating in his painting?

▶ What purpose do you think the face jugs served?

Aesthetic Perception

Design Awareness Think about the facial expressions you have seen people make. What feelings do they communicate?

Using Facial Distortion

Distortion is based on the art principle of proportion. **Distortion** is a deviation from normal or expected proportions. Artists use distortion to express personal feelings and to communicate emotions. Distortion is a powerful means of expression and can convey feelings or meanings that normal proportions cannot.

Think about other places where you have seen distortion. Cartoonists often use facial distortion in their art to emphasize character traits. If you have ever seen caricatures of famous people you have probably noticed that one feature is often exaggerated or distorted. Distortion is also commonly used in masks. Many cultures distort the features on masks used for religious or celebratory purposes.

Practice

Work in groups to act out an emotion using facial expressions.

1. Work in small groups. Your teacher will select the name of an emotion or expression from an envelope for your group to perform.

2. Look at the name of the emotion or expression. As a group, practice exaggerating the facial expression assigned.

3. Take turns with the other groups in your class performing the emotions or expressions. Can you correctly identify the emotions expressed?

Think about which features the student artists distorted in their face pots.

Creative Expression

Create a clay face jug, using a distorted feature.

1. Create various sketches of a face jug and select one. Look at your selected sketch, and then make a clay sphere. Gently pat your form, turning it in your hands to make it even all around. Flatten the bottom to sit upright.

2. Pinch out a spout at the top of your form, but do not make a hole. Lightly draw the facial features.

3. Form and attach the features using the scoring method. Make the eyes from small balls of clay, and make the lids from small coils of clay.

4. Use a pencil to pierce a hole in the spout as you support it with your fingers. Add color with glaze.

Art Criticism

Describe Describe the expression on your face jug.

Analyze What forms did you use? How did you distort a feature?

Interpret What emotion or mood does your face jug communicate?

Decide Were you successful in creating a face jug using distortion? Explain.

Lesson 4 Figure Distortion

Look at the works of art on these pages. Notice the extreme proportions these artists used. Alberto Giacometti originally made his figures from wire covered in plaster. He was part of a group of artists known as surrealists, who were inspired by dreams and fantasy. *Dancing in Colombia* is typical of Colombian-born artist Fernando Botero. His figures have plump proportions, which he calls "plasticity." Not only his figures are rounded, but so are all of the other objects in his paintings. Each of these works of art is an example of figure distortion.

▲ **Alberto Giacometti.** (Swiss). *City Square.* 1948.

Bronze. $8\frac{1}{2} \times 25\frac{3}{4} \times 17\frac{1}{4}$ inches (21.59 × 65.41 × 43.82 cm.). Museum of Modern Art, New York, New York.

 Art History and Culture

As a child, Giacometti wanted to be an illustrator. Botero had a job as an illustrator. In what ways do these works of art remind you of cartoons?

▲ **Fernando Botero.**
(Colombian). *Dancing in Colombia.* 1980.

Oil on canvas. 74 × 91 inches
(187.96 × 231.14 cm.). The
Metropolitan Museum of Art,
New York, New York.

Study the two works of art to learn how figure distortion is used.

▶ Which figures are elongated, or stretched?

▶ How did Botero distort the people in *Dancing in Colombia?*

▶ Describe the negative space around and between the figures in *City Square*. How does this affect the feeling of the work?

▶ Describe the images and emotions that come to mind when you view each work of art.

Aesthetic Perception

Design Awareness Think of a time when you were part of a crowd but did not know anyone or just did not want to be there. What did you seem to notice the most?

Using Figure Distortion

In the last lesson you learned that artists use distortion to express feelings and emotions. Artwork created with distorted figures often produces intense feelings in the viewer. Sometimes the distortions create feelings of love and happiness; other times they create feelings of fear or loneliness.

Artists communicate these moods or feelings so their works can be better understood by viewers. An artist can elongate or lengthen a form, as Giacometti did in *City Square.* Other artists, like Botero, inflate or enlarge a figure to create a result that is monumental, large, or imposing. The figures in *Dancing in Colombia* were created with exaggerated proportions. Exaggeration is a form of distortion. **Exaggeration** is an increase or enlargement of an object beyond what is expected or normal. When artists exaggerate things, they might make them extra long or extra wide. Artists can also bend, warp, twist, and deform parts, or all, of the human body to create figure distortions.

Practice

Look through comic strips for examples of figure distortion.

1. Work in groups of three or four. Look through comic strips and collect images of distorted figures.

2. Create a grid on the board as a class. Use these categories: Elongated/Stretched, Exaggerated/Enlarged, Twisted/Bent.

3. Share collected images of comic strips with the class. Categorize and record each of the comic-strip images on the grid. Which type of distortion was used most often? Which was used least often?

◀ **Brianna Ruch.**
Age 12.

Think about how the student artist distorted this figure.

Creative Expression

Use the computer to distort a photograph.

1. Use a digital camera, and take several photographs of a family member or friend. Choose one or two of your photographs.

2. Begin by loading the image into the computer. If you have regular photographs, scan them into the computer.

3. Use a draw or paint program to create a copy of the image, and then save it. Use a variety of tools on the menu to create a distortion of the image.

4. Add textures to the background or alter the colors. Title and save your work.

Art Criticism

Describe What tools did you use to distort your image?

Analyze Describe the textures and/or color schemes you used to alter your image. What type of distortion did you use?

Interpret How did distortion affect the mood of your work? Explain.

Decide Were you successful in creating figure distortion in your artwork? Explain.

Realistic Scale

▲ **Mosche Safdie.** (Israeli).
Habitat. 1967.
Concrete. Montreal, Canada.

Look closely at the two works of art on these pages. Notice how both artists created artwork using realistic scale. Mosche Safdie designed *Habitat* for the Expo in Montreal in 1967. Each of the single cubes is a precast concrete unit. The units were mass-produced, then transported to the site and assembled. The units vary in size and have different interiors. Julia Russell painted *Leonardo da Vinci's Chair* for a fundraiser for the arts. The work was so successful that she began to create compositions based on her favorite artists for other chairs. Russell studies an artist's style and artwork, creates a detailed composition, and then transfers it onto a specially prepared chair. After she draws the details, she uses acrylic paint to complete the work.

 **Art History and Culture**

Examine these pieces of art. Do they remind you of other cultures?

Study the two works of art to learn how artists use realistic scale.

▶ How tall do you think you would be in relation to Russell's chair? On what are you basing your guess?

▶ How large do you think Safdie's buildings are? What objects in the photograph give you a clue about their size?

▶ What do you think Safdie used as the basis for the building's dimensions? Why?

▶ Would you want to live in *Habitat*? Explain your answer.

▶ If you owned Julia Russell's chair, what room would you place it in and how would you use it?

◀ **Julia Russell.** (American). *Leonardo da Vinci Chair.* Twentieth century.
....
Private Collection.

Aesthetic Perception

Design Awareness Think of a time when you sat in a chair that was too small or too big. Share with the class how it felt to sit in that chair.

Using Realistic Scale

Scale, like proportion, is about size relationships. **Scale** refers to size as measured against a standard reference. An average-sized person is a good scale reference. If you saw a professional basketball player standing with other basketball players, he would not look tall. However, if that same person were in a crowd of fans, he would look very tall. With scale, you can compare the size of various objects in relation to objects you know are always a consistent size.

One type of scale is the actual size of an artwork. This is realistic scale. Realistic scale is used in a work of art in which everything fits together and makes sense in relation to size. Often this size relation is based on averages or standards. Objects that people use for daily living are made to scale based on average human proportions. Chairs, tables, buildings, clothing, and dinnerware are just a few examples of objects that are based on realistic scale.

Practice

Look through a magazine to find examples of realistic scale.

1. Collect images of three different people. Cut out the images so that you have removed most of the excess paper from around the people.

2. On a separate sheet of paper, glue the pictures of the three people so that there is a space next to each one.

3. Use a ruler to find the height and width of each person. Write your measurements next to each of your cut-out people. Save your work for the Creative Expression activity.

◀ **Lauren Shaw.**
Age 12.

Think about whether a child or an adult would use this chair.

 **Creative Expression**

How does a designer decide on the size of a piece of furniture? Use images from a magazine to design a chair, using realistic scale.

1. Look at the list of rooms and images in your Art Journal. Select one of the people from the Practice activity as your client.

2. Begin planning a chair for your client. Think about where it will be used and the image you will use for your design. Create several sketches until you make one you like.

3. Use a pencil and a ruler to draw your chair to scale.

4. Use color pencils to add details and to complete your design.

Art Criticism

Describe Who is your chair for? What object did you use as the basis for your design?

Analyze Describe your color scheme. Explain how you used realistic scale.

Interpret Why do you think your client would like your chair?

Decide Were you able to design a chair successfully for a specific person, using realistic scale? Explain.

Unrealistic Scale

▲ **Salvador Dalí.** (Spanish).
Persistence of Memory.
1931.

Oil on canvas. $9\frac{1}{2}$ × 13 inches
(24.13 × 33.02 cm.). The Museum
of Modern Art, New York, New York.

Look at the works of art on these pages to learn more about scale. Pablo Picasso was asked by Chicago architect William Hartmann to produce a monumental sculpture to be placed in front of the Civic Center. Picasso, who never visited Chicago or the United States, gave his work as a gift to the people of Chicago. His sculpture came to be called the *Chicago Picasso.* Salvador Dalí painted the dreamlike images of *Persistence of Memory* during the peak of surrealism. Surrealism emphasized art in which dreams, fantasy, and the subconscious served as inspiration for artists. Dalí's images were painted in a precise, realistic manner and include commonplace objects. He distorted the objects so they do not look real. Notice how he placed unrelated objects together. The landscape contains strange objects that do not seem to belong there and appear to be made of unexpected materials.

🏺 Art History and Culture

Both Dalí and Picasso were born in Spain. Do either of their works of art remind you of Spain or of something Spanish?

◀ **Pablo Picasso.** (Spanish).
Chicago Picasso. 1967.
. . . .
Steel. 50 feet tall (15.24 meters).
Civic Center Plaza, Chicago, Illinois.

Study the two works of art to learn how unrealistic scale is used.

▶ Describe the unusual objects in *Persistence of Memory*.

▶ What is unusual about the size of the objects in *Persistence of Memory?*

▶ Would the *Chicago Picasso* have the same effect if it were a tabletop sculpture? Why?

▶ How do you think it would feel to walk under the *Chicago Picasso?*

▶ What would it be like to walk into Dalí's painting? What sounds might you hear? What do you think the clocks would feel like if you could touch them?

Aesthetic Perception

Design Awareness Imagine that you are only six inches tall. How would the objects around you look?

Using Unrealistic Scale

One type of scale is the actual size of an object or artwork in relation to human scale. When a person stands next to an artwork you can see the difference in scale. A second type of scale is the size relationship of the objects or elements within a design. Sometimes the objects or elements relate to one another based on realistic scale, for example, the size of the furniture in relation to the people in an artwork. At other times, the objects or elements relate to one another based on unrealistic scale.

Unrealistic scale is used when an artist makes size relationships that do not make sense. For example, making a small object, such as a button, larger than the hand holding it creates unrealistic scale. Artists use unrealistic scale in both two- and three-dimensional artwork. Variation in scale within an artwork can change the work's total impact. When unrealistic scale is used, it creates dreamlike or fantasy qualities in the work. The effect often captures the viewer's attention because it is so different from what is normally seen.

Practice

Look for examples of unrealistic scale.

1. Work in groups of three or four. Look through your textbook and the **Large Prints** for examples of unrealistic scale. Unrealistic scale can be either smaller or larger than normal.

2. Read the measurements in the credit lines. Select the dimensions of one of the works of art and measure that area on a table, a wall, or the floor. Use tape to show the dimensions.

3. Share your measurements with the class.

Think about how the student artist used unrealistic scale in this collage.

🎨 Creative Expression

Create a surrealistic collage, showing unrealistic scale.

1. Begin by sketching several designs. Select your best one. Look at the collected cutouts in your Art Journal and place them on the table. Select three of the images to use in your collage.

2. Look through magazines to find at least four examples of natural elements, such as trees and rocks. Cut these out.

3. Lightly transfer your sketch onto paper. Combine your collected images to create a surreal collage.

4. Use oil pastels to add color and complete your work.

⚠️❓ Art Criticism

Describe What images did you use?

Analyze Describe how you used unrealistic scale.

Interpret How does your use of unrealistic scale affect the mood of your work? Explain.

Decide Were you successful in creating a collage, using unrealistic scale? Explain.

▲ **Leonardo da Vinci.** (Italian).
Ginevra de' Benci. c. 1474.

Oil on canvas. $16\frac{13}{16} \times 14\frac{9}{16}$ inches (42.7 × 36.98 cm.).
National Gallery of Art, Washington, D.C.

Art Criticism | Critical Thinking

Describe **What do you see?**

During this step you will collect information about the subject of the work.

► Describe the woman, including her clothing, her hair, and the features of her face.

► What do you see behind Ginevra?

Analyze **How is this work organized?**

Think about how the artist used the elements and principles of art.

► Did Leonardo da Vinci use realistic proportions or distortion?

► Measure the face and describe how da Vinci used facial proportions.

► Describe the scale of the background in relation to Ginevra.

Interpret **What does the artwork say?**

Combine clues you collected during your description and analysis with your personal experiences to find out what this painting is about.

► What is unusual about Ginevra's eyes and mouth?

► What feelings does her face express?

► How does da Vinci's use of proportion affect the expressive quality of the painting?

► If Leonardo da Vinci were alive today, whose portrait do you think he would choose to paint? Why?

Decide **What do you think about the work?**

Use all the information you have gathered to decide why this is a successful work of art.

► Is this work successful because it is realistic, because it is well organized, or because it conveys a message?

Show What You Know

Answer these questions on a separate sheet of paper.

❶ A _____ is a comparison of size between two things.
   A. ratio
   B. scale
   C. scheme

❷ _____ is an increase or enlargement beyond what is expected or normal.
   A. Proportion
   B. Exaggeration
   C. Elaboration

❸ The principle of art concerned with the size relationship of one part to another is called _____.
   A. proportion
   B. distortion
   C. scale

❹ _____ refers to size as measured against a standard reference.
   A. The central axis
   B. Ratio
   C. Scale

❺ _____ is a deviation from normal or expected proportions.
   A. Realistic scale
   B. Distortion
   C. Variation

CAREERS IN ART
Graphic Design

Graphic designers create a pleasing layout with text and graphics. They use a variety of print, electronic, and film media.

Book designers are responsible for designing the outsides and insides of books. A book designer wants the outside of a book to be as unique as it possibly can be, and the focus is usually on color. On the inside, the book is designed to be well organized and easy for the reader to follow.

Font designers usually study and practice for about seven years before they are established. Their skill is acquired through study of the visual forms and practice in making them. Most font designers work individually. Designing a font can take several months to several years. A *font* is a complete set of letters, numbers, and symbols, all of the same style.

Packaging designers have the job of making the outside of a product grab the buyer's attention. They do this by combining colors, graphics, unique shapes, and any other eye-catching designs they think will help sell the product.

▲ Book designer

Proportion and Distortion in Theatre

By wearing different masks, Robert Faust can make himself into many characters. He surprises everyone with his odd postures and the strange features of his masks. He alters the proportion of his human form by making some masks huge and some very small. He also exaggerates the shapes of noses, eyes, and mouths.

What to Do Create a character by exaggerating the way they walk.

A character can be defined by exaggerating the way they walk. You can change the size of the steps, give the walk a rhythm, and alter the speed. Posture also affects the way one walks Also, the emotion of the character is important.

1. Try walking in various exaggerated ways. Take very large steps, then tiny ones. Walk slowly, then quickly. Walk in a stiff, then loose, way. Walk as if you were curious about everything, then disinterested.

2. Think of a character you would like to show. Explore how this character might walk. Exaggerate the movement so that it clearly shows the posture, attitude, emotion, and size of the character.

3. Share your character and walk with a partner or small group. Discuss the traits of each character.

▲ Robert Faust. "The Mask Messenger."

 **Art Criticism**

Describe Describe the character you created.

Analyze How did you exaggerate the walk to clearly show the traits of your character?

Interpret How did it feel to walk as your character?

Decide Were you successful in creating a character and a walk that communicated his/her traits?

Variety, Harmony, and Unity

▲ **Paul Gauguin.** (French).
The Brooding Woman (Te Faaturuma). 1891.
Oil on canvas. $35\frac{15}{16} \times 27\frac{1}{16}$ inches (91.2 × 68.7 cm.).
Worcester Art Museum, Worcester, Massachusetts.

Variety, harmony, and unity are used by artists to arrange the art elements in both two- and three-dimensional art.

Paul Gauguin is best known in the art world as a rebel. He used color and shape to create unconventional works of far-off lands and primitive life. He traveled often and settled on the tropical island of Tahiti, where he produced his most famous works. Notice how Gauguin used color to express emotion in *The Brooding Woman.*

Artists use **variety** to show differences or contrasts in a work of art.

▶ What different objects do you see?

▶ Describe the contrasting colors, lines, and shapes.

Artists can stress the similarities of separate but related parts in an artwork by using **harmony.**

▶ How did Gauguin relate the outside scene to the interior?

▶ What element of this painting gives it a feeling of oneness or wholeness?

Unity is the feeling of oneness that artists create in their works of art.

▶ What about this work makes all the pieces look like they belong?

In This Unit you will learn how artists use variety and harmony. You will create works of art using a variety of media. You will create a weaving using two-dimensional decorations and a sculpture using a three-dimensional form. You will also learn how artists use unity to bring together art elements and objects.

Here are the topics you will study:
▶ Variety
▶ Harmony
▶ Weaving
▶ Unity

Paul Gauguin
(1848–1903)

Paul Gauguin began painting as a hobby. In 1883 he quit his job as a stockbroker and decided to paint full-time. Gauguin used color and shape in new and exciting ways. *The Brooding Woman* shows a scene from the South Seas, where Gauguin spent the later part of his life. *The Brooding Woman* was painted during the first of Gauguin's two visits to Tahiti. It shows Gauguin's use of bright colors and simple forms. He considered this painting to be among his best. French impressionist artist Edgar Degas owned this painting and several other works by Gauguin.

Variety through Line, Shape, and Color

Look at the works of art on these pages. Notice that both works of art include a variety of lines, shapes, and colors. Lee Bennion painted an image of Adah, the youngest of her three daughters, standing in the window in her pajamas. The colors and lines add interest to the painting. Bustion's serigraph expresses the joy and excitement of a festival. Bustion used a variety of shapes and patterns, which makes his work interesting to view. See how many hidden masks you can find in this composition.

◀ **Nathaniel Bustion.** (American).
Bo Bo Festival Series 3. Twentieth century.
....
Serigraph. $18\frac{1}{2} \times 12$ inches (47×30.5 cm.).
Collection of the artist.

 Art History and Culture

Color is a dominant element in the artwork of both Bustion and Bennion. What other artists use color as a dominant element?

▲ **Lee Bennion.** (American).
Snow Queen, Portrait of Adah. 1992.
••
Oil on canvas. 48 × 36 inches (121.9 × 91.4 cm.).
Springville Museum of Art, Springville, Utah.

Study the two paintings closely to learn about variety.

▶ Describe the shapes, colors, and patterns in Bustion's serigraph.

▶ Describe the shapes, colors, and patterns in *Snow Queen, Portrait of Adah.*

▶ Compare the shapes in the two works of art.

▶ In what ways did both artists use contrast?

Aesthetic Perception

Design Awareness Think of a window display you have seen at a store. What did you notice about the items on display?

Using Variety Through Line, Shape, and Color

Think about walking through a shopping center. The displays, signs, and the ways the items are displayed are all varied. If every store looked the same or sold the same product, the stores' owners would have a hard time staying in business. People like to have choices and are attracted to differences. Owners and managers put a great deal of time and effort into creating variety in their stores.

Artists use variety as well. **Variety** is the principle of art that relates to differences or contrasts. A work of art that is all the same is dull and will not hold the viewer's attention for long. Think about a painting that has only one color. Unless there is another art element in it, the painting will not be interesting to look at. Variety is achieved by adding something different to a design to provide a break in the repetition.

Lines, shapes, and colors are three of the art elements that are used to create variety in a work of art.

Practice

Create a pattern out of a piece of paper.

1. Fold a sheet of paper in half and draw a triangle on the fold, leaving room above and below it. Cut out the shape and open the sheet of paper. What shape do you see?

2. Fold the paper in half again and cut out another shape. What happens to the shape when you open the paper? Fold and cut out your last shape. Notice the variety of the pattern.

◀ **Ashley Guzini.**
Age 11.

Think about how the student artist used variety in this collage.

Creative Expression

Choose either an animal or a person to represent in a paper collage. Use a variety of lines, shapes, and colors in your composition.

1. Select your best sketch from your Art Journal. Then select a colored sheet of paper for your background.

2. Begin by cutting out the shape of the person or animal from paper whose color contrasts with your background color.

3. Use a variety of colors and shapes to cut out objects for your environment. Overlap your shapes to make them more interesting.

4. Glue your arrangement in place. Use a felt-tip marker to make a variety of repeated lines to complete your collage.

Art Criticism

Describe What subject matter and environment did you use for your collage?

Analyze Describe the lines, shapes, and colors you used to create variety.

Interpret How does your use of variety affect the mood of your work? Explain.

Decide Do you think you were successful in arranging lines, shapes, and colors to create variety in your collage? Explain.

Lesson 2 Variety Through Contrast

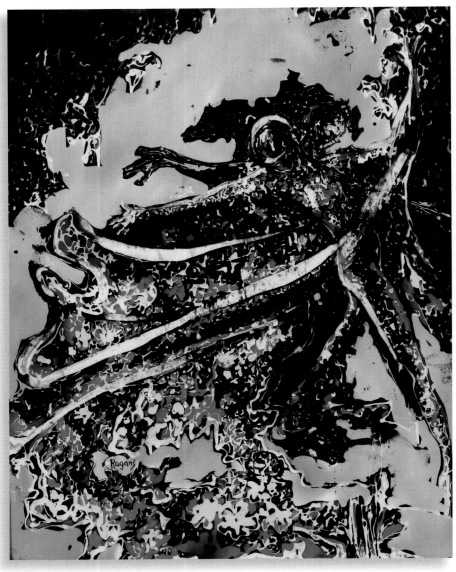

▲ **Rosalind Ragans.** (American).
Pas de Deux. 2003.

Batik on cotton. 36 × 24 inches (91.4 × 61 cm.).
Private collection.

Look at the two works of art on these pages. Both of these works include variety through contrasts of value. As a child, Rosalind Ragans suffered from polio and was paralyzed on her right side. She regained nearly all the movement in her body with the help of therapy. In *Pas de Deux,* Ragans was able to express her mind's ability to dance, even though her body could not. In *Chuska,* there are images of five horses running in front of a mountain range. It is hard for the viewer to take his or her eyes away from the dark horses because of the contrast in value with the light area around the horses.

 Art History and Culture

What other American artists have you studied whose works of art have subject matter similar to these works of art?

▲ **Paul Brach.** (American).
Chuska. 1982.

Oil and gold leaf on canvas. 50 × 60 inches
(127 × 152.4 cm.). Private collection.

Study how contrast is used to create variety in these
two-dimensional works of art.

▶ Where are the dark values in each work of art?

▶ Where are the lightest values in each work?

▶ What is mysterious about both artists' use of value?

▶ What type of music do you think the figures in *Pas de
Deux* are dancing to? What sounds would you hear if
you were standing in Brach's painting?

Aesthetic Perception

Seeing Like an Artist Think about a sunset and how the sky changes as
night approaches. What kind of contrast do you notice?

Using Variety Through Contrast

Have you ever noticed that when a film is playing in a darkened theater, it is hard to turn your head away from the screen? This is because several things are happening. A story is unfolding, and the light from the screen contrasts with the darkened theater. The contrast of light against dark adds variety to the environment. **Variety** is the principle of art that relates to differences or contrasts.

An artist often uses contrast to keep the viewer's attention on a certain part of an artwork. This is done in a manner similar to that of a lighted movie screen in a darkened theater. Sometimes the contrast in value is subtle, as in Brach's *Chuska,* which is made up of values of red. Other times the contrast of value is very noticeable. *Pas de Deux* by Rosalind Ragans is an example of an artist's use of high contrast. Ragans placed a light value of a color against a dark value of another color.

Practice

Create variety through color contrast in a black-and-white image.

1. Cut out two black-and-white images from a newspaper showing a range of values. Glue the images next to each other on a background sheet of paper. Use a dot of glue in each corner of the images to keep them from tearing.

2. Add a single color to only one of your images. Color in two areas you want to emphasize.

◄ **Jacqueline Mayo.**
Age 12.

Think about how the student artist created variety in this photograph.

Creative Expression

What theme will you use for your hand-colored photograph? Hand-color a photograph to create variety.

1. Decide on a theme and take several black-and-white photographs.

2. Look at your developed images carefully. Choose one or two photographs that show a range of gray values. Put these aside to hand-color.

3. Select a third image for practice. See Technique Tip, Hand-Coloring a Photograph. Experiment with the various techniques.

4. Add variety to your two selected images by adding color to one or three areas in each photograph. Use one hand-coloring technique you like for each image.

Art Criticism

Describe What images did you choose? Why?

Analyze Describe the techniques you used to add variety to each photograph.

Interpret How does the hand-coloring affect the mood of each photograph?

Decide Do you think you were successful in creating variety in your photographs? Explain.

Lesson 3 Harmony in Two-Dimensional Art

▲ **Grandma Moses.**
(American). *Mt. Nebo on the Hill.* 1940 or earlier.

Embroidery yarn on fabric.
10 × 14 inches (25.4 × 35.6 cm.).
Galerie St. Etienne, New York,
New York.

Look at the two works of art on these pages. Anna Mary Robertson, known as Grandma Moses, is most famous for painted landscapes based on her childhood experiences. Before she began painting, she created original needlepoint pieces depicting scenes of her home and community. When she was well into her seventies and her eyesight began to fail, she turned to painting. Moses was the originator of the style known as memory painting. *Woman's Headcloth* is handwoven. Some women in hot climates fold cloths like these on top of their heads and use them as sunshades. These textiles can also be used as carrying cloths for babies and various items. The figures on the headcloths vary in size and shape, which makes them unique pieces of art.

 Art History and Culture

Embroidery and other fiber and needlework arts most likely originated in Asia and the Middle East.

◀ **Artist unknown.**
(Guatemala). *Woman's Headcloth.* c. 1935–1945.
· ·
Cotton, silk, and wool.
50 × 44 inches (127 × 111.8 cm.).
Dallas Museum of Art, Dallas, Texas.

Study how harmony is used in both works of art.

▶ Describe any repeated lines, shapes, colors, and textures you see in each work of art.

▶ Describe any one area in either artwork that seems to stand out.

▶ Which art element in *Mt. Nebo on the Hill* ties the work together?

▶ Which work of art do you think was more difficult to create? Explain.

Aesthetic Perception

Design Awareness Look at the clothing you have on. What about it makes it look like the separate pieces go together?

Using Harmony in Two-Dimensional Art

You have probably heard the term *harmony* used in connection with music. When voices harmonize, they blend together to create a unified sound. Artists use this same concept, but instead of combining sounds, they combine the art elements. **Harmony** is the principle of art that creates unity by stressing similarities of separate but related parts. Artists create harmony in two-dimensional works of art by repeating shapes, colors, and textures. Harmony can also occur when the spaces between different shapes, colors, and/or textures are even.

Look at Grandma Moses's embroidery again. Even though there is a variety of shapes, lines, and yarn textures, the use of cool colors and neutral colors unifies the separate parts. The purples in the hillside and sky, the greens in the grass and plants, and the grays, browns, black, and white in the buildings and trees create harmony.

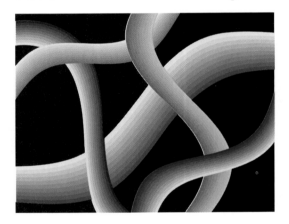
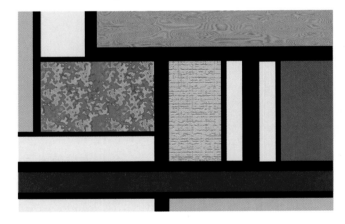

Practice

Practice using various embroidery techniques.

1. Look at the Techniques Tips for embroidery.
2. With a permanent marker draw one line of any type on your burlap. Draw any type of shape no larger than a quarter.
3. Use the running, back, or outline stitch on the line you made. Practice the satin stitch on the shape you made. If you have time, you may want to try another embroidery technique.

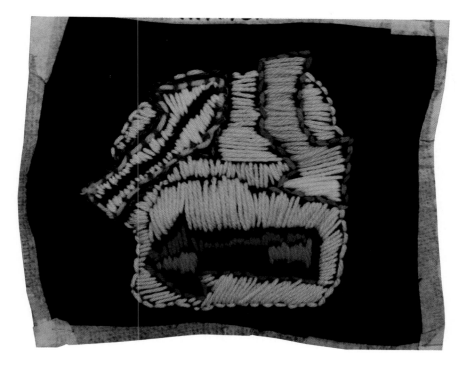

Think about which art element the student artist used in this artwork to create harmony.

Creative Expression

Think about an important event in your life. Create a harmonious embroidery based on this event.

1. Look over your planned sketch in your Art Journal or create a new one. Use a light piece of chalk to transfer your design to the burlap. Make your image large, and keep your design simple.

2. Use masking tape to tape around the edges of the burlap before you begin stitching. This will keep it from unraveling.

3. Look at your practice embroidery piece and the Technique Tips on page 214. Outline your image first using either a running, back, or outline stitch. Use a contrasting color of yarn and a satin stitch to complete your work. Make sure you have used at least one art element in your embroidery to create harmony.

Art Criticism

Describe Describe the image you used in your embroidery. What embroidery techniques did you use?

Analyze List the lines, shapes, colors, and textures you used in your embroidery. Which element did you use to create harmony? Explain.

Interpret Give your completed work a descriptive title.

Decide Do you feel your embroidery piece is a success? Explain.

Harmony in Three-Dimensional Art

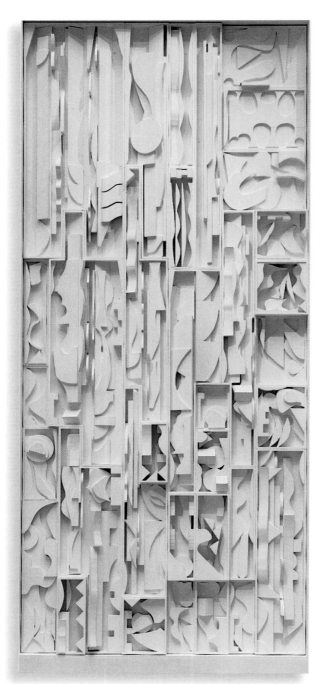

Look at the works of art on these pages. Many of the wood forms Louise Nevelson used in *White Vertical Water* are similar to those she grew up with in her father's lumber yard. She gathered the discarded wood pieces for her sculptures from renovations of Victorian homes. She then arranged the various pieces in boxes. As she was stacking boxes in her studio to make more room, she noticed a sculptural form. Like Nevelson, Randy Ellett was influenced by his surroundings. Working as a forklift driver, he would move objects around a warehouse on wooden pallets. The writing and images on the pallets intrigued him and were the inspiration for *National Parts*. Notice how the various images are arranged. Each individual shape represents one pallet.

◀ **Louise Nevelson.** (Russian/American).
White Vertical Water. 1972.
. . . .
Painted wood. 26 sections. 216 × 108 inches overall (548.6 × 274.3 cm.).
Solomon R. Guggenheim Museum, New York, New York.

 Art History and Culture

Both Nevelson and Ellet used geometric elements in their sculptures. Can you name another artist who did the same?

Study how Nevelson and Ellett used harmony in their works of art.

▶ Describe the types of lines and shapes used in each artwork.

▶ Is there any one element in each artwork that seems to stand out?

▶ How do you think these works were assembled?

▶ Why do you think Nevelson named her work *White Vertical Water*? Why do you think Ellett named his work *National Parts*?

◀ **Randy Ellett.** (American).
National Parts. 1996.
....
Wooden pallets. $73\frac{5}{8} \times 15\frac{1}{2} \times 2\frac{3}{8}$ inches
($187 \times 39.4 \times 5.4$ cm.). Collection of the artist.

Aesthetic Perception

Design Awareness Think about how the various parts of playground equipment are put together.

Using Harmony in Three-Dimensional Assemblages

Harmony is the principle of art that creates unity by stressing similarities of separate but related parts. Artists create harmony in three-dimensional works of art by repeating shapes, colors, or similar materials. When an artist works with an **assemblage,** a variety of objects put together to create one complete piece, he or she uses harmony.

Notice how Louise Nevelson used a variety of wooden objects in *White Vertical Water.* Even though there is a variety of shapes and forms, the use of white and the rectangular boxes unify the separate pieces. The repetition of rectangular shapes harmonizes the various words and images in *National Parts.*

Practice

Work as a class or table group to harmonize a variety of objects.

1. Look around your classroom. What colors, shapes, textures, and materials do you see?

2. Decide which art element you will use. Gather several objects from around the room that are made up of this element. For example, you might choose all wood objects or objects that are geometric shapes.

3. Arrange the collected objects. What do you notice?

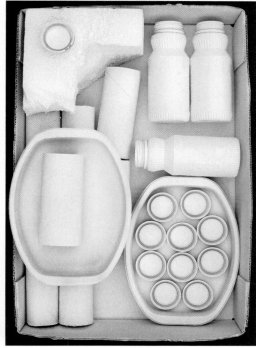

◄ **Bobby Braswell.**
Age 11.

Think about how the student artist used harmony to bring together the various objects in this work of art.

Creative Expression

Collect a variety of discarded objects and make a harmonious group assemblage.

1. Look over the list of recycled objects in your Art Journal and try to collect several of the objects.

2. Begin by arranging the objects in the box. None of the objects should stick out beyond one inch from the box's edge. Think about repeating similar shapes in one area of the box and using different shapes in another area.

3. Once you have arranged your objects, glue them in place. Use one harmonious color to paint all of the assemblages of your group members. Arrange the individual works to create one or two harmonious sculptures.

Art Criticism

Describe List the objects you used in your assemblage.

Analyze List the lines, shapes, colors, and textures used in the group sculpture. Which element was used to create harmony?

Interpret Imagine that you are an art critic and write a review of the sculpture for a newspaper.

Decide Do you feel your assemblage is a success? Is the group sculpture a success? Explain.

Unity in Weaving

Look at the two woven works of art on these pages. *Basket* was created through weaving. Louisa Keyser was a member of the Washoe tribe of the American Northwest. The method of weaving used is called *coiling* because the basket was woven in one continuous coil. Washoe baskets are watertight and were used to carry various items. *Basket* is based on a *degikup (deh gee' kup)*, a small, round basket used for ceremonies. In Indonesia, a ceremonial hanging is called a *palepai (pah lee' peye)*. A *palepai* can be hung during ceremonies for important life events, and only by titled members of the nobility. *Ceremonial Hanging* includes images of animals carrying riders, trees, and a ship.

▲ **Louisa Keyser (Dat So La Lee).**
(Washoe/North American).
Basket. c. 1917–1918.

Redbud and braken fern. 12 × 16¼ inches (30.5 × 41.3 cm.). Philbrook Museum of Art, Tulsa, Oklahoma.

 Art History and Culture

Do you notice any similarities between the Washoe basket and the Indonesian ceremonial hanging? Explain.

▲ **Artist unknown.** (Indonesia).
Ceremonial Hanging. c. 1900.

Cotton and metal wrapped yarns.
$24\frac{3}{4} \times 95\frac{3}{4}$ inches (61.6 × 243.2 cm.).
Dallas Museum of Art, Dallas, Texas.

Study the works of art to see how unity is used in weaving.

▶ Which art elements create variety in each weaving?

▶ Which art elements create harmony in each weaving?

▶ How are all the images brought together to make
Ceremonial Hanging work?

▶ How did Keyser balance all the different parts in *Basket*?

Aesthetic Perception

Design Awareness Think about a patterned blanket you have seen before.
What about this blanket gave it the feeling of oneness?

Using Unity in Weaving

Unity is oneness. For example, the separate states are brought together or unified as one United States. In art, **unity** is the feeling of wholeness or oneness that is achieved by properly using the elements and principles of art. Unity is created when the art principles of variety and harmony work together.

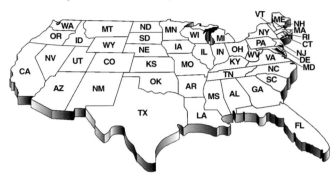

In a weaving, the separate parts relate to one another to make the whole weaving. Various lines, shapes, and colors are woven together. One way in which variety and harmony work together to create unity or oneness in a weaving is the very technique of weaving. Most weaving is done on a loom. The shape and consistent technique of weaving on a loom unify the whole. Notice the image of the weaving loom and tools below. These are what a weaver needs to created a completely unified weaving.

Practice

Discuss how unity occurs in architecture.

1. In a small group, create a list of all of the elements or parts needed to construct a house.

2. Answer these questions: Why do you need each part? How do each of these separate parts fit together?

3. Share your answers with the class. Discuss how variety and harmony are used together to create unity in architecture.

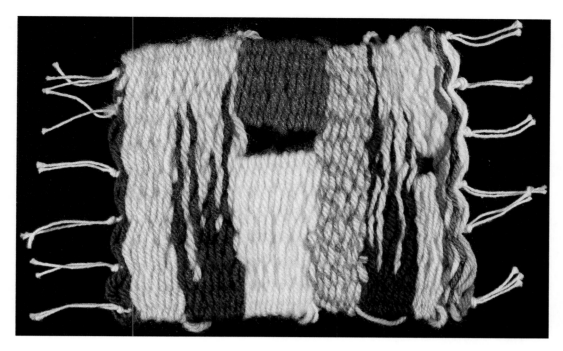

◀ **Bethany Ullrich.**
Age 11.

Think about how the student artist used unity in this weaving.

Creative Expression

How can you use unity in your cardboard-loom weaving?

1. Prepare your loom following the Technique Tips. Look at your loom design in your Art Journal. Select a yarn and attach it to the first warp string.

2. Begin by using the tabby (basket) weave for the first few rows. Your teacher will demonstrate other weaving techniques you can use.

3. Look at your sketch and try to follow your plan. Make any adjustments to your design.

4. When finished, take your weaving off the loom. Turn it over, and cut the warp strings across the center. Cut two strings at a time. Gently lift the top two strings and knot them together. The knot should be close to the weaving. Repeat this process until all the strings are cut and tied.

Art Criticism

Describe What weaving techniques did you use? List the colors you used in your weaving.

Analyze Describe how variety and harmony were used to create unity in your weaving.

Interpret If you could enlarge your weaving, what size would you make it? What would it be used for?

Decide Were you successful in using unity in your weaving? Explain.

Unity in Three-Dimensional Art

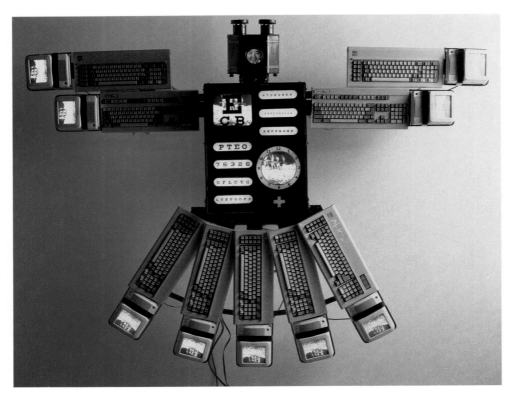

▲ **Nam June Paik.** (Korean/American).
Eagle Eye. 1996.

Antique slide projector and eye chart, transparency of
the artist, aluminum, nine computer keyboards, neon,
nine Sony 5-inch televisions model FDT-5BX5, two KEC
9-inch televisions model 9BND, and DVD.
$66\frac{11}{16} \times 86\frac{3}{8} \times 24\frac{1}{2}$ inches (169.4 × 219.4 × 62.2 cm.).
Ackland Art Museum, Chapel Hill, North Carolina.

Look at the forms of the sculptures on these pages. Nam
June Paik is considered the first artist to explore the area of
video art. Paik created *Eagle Eye* based on the Native
American thunderbird. He combined old technology—a
slide projector and an eye chart—with the newer
technology of computers, television, and DVDs. A portrait
of Paik is in the work; he is the eagle, blending old
technology with new. Christina Lemon is a professor of
jewelry and design at Georgia Southern University. She
works primarily with silver and gold, although she uses a
variety of materials with her students. By using simple
shapes and contrasting colors in *Mask Brooch,* Lemon was
able to suggest the feeling of a mask without making a
symmetrical face. Both artists use unity in their three-
dimensional forms.

 Art History and Culture

When creating works of art, both Nam June Paik and Christina Lemon look to
other cultures for inspiration.

Study the works of art to see how unity is used in three-dimensional art.

▶ Which elements or objects create variety in each artwork?

▶ Which elements or objects create harmony in each work?

▶ How did Nam June Paik bring all the pieces together to make *Eagle Eye* work?

▶ How did Lemon balance all the different parts in *Mask Brooch*?

◀ **Christina Lemon.** (American). *Mask Brooch.* 2003.
. . . .
Sterling silver and 18-karat gold laminate. $2\frac{1}{2} \times 1$ inch (6.4 × 2.5 cm.). Collection of the artist.

 Aesthetic Perception

Design Awareness Think about a computer system, a music system, or a media center. Describe the different parts that are needed to complete the system.

Using Unity in Three-Dimensional Forms

In art, **unity** is the feeling of wholeness or oneness that is achieved by properly using the elements and principles of art. Unity is oneness. It brings order to a work of art. It helps the viewer concentrate on the image as a whole. When an artwork does not have unity, it is very difficult to concentrate on because each part demands the viewer's separate attention. It is like trying to read a story when a lawn mower is running and a dog is barking. To create unity, an artist adjusts the parts so that they work together. This is done by using the art principles of variety and harmony together. When an artist uses unity, he or she harmonizes the variety, or different elements or objects, by making them relate to one another.

By combining like objects, or things that relate, and organizing them in an understandable manner, an artist creates unity. Look at the sets of objects below. Even though these are not art objects their arrangement and dependency on each other make them unified sets.

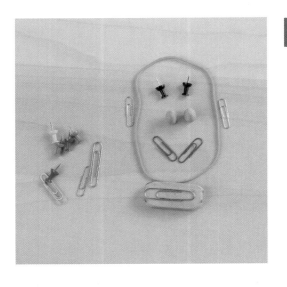

Practice

Try creating a face or human form from a variety of objects.

1. Pull an assortment of objects from your desk, book-bag, or pockets. Look around the room for small objects as well.

2. Once you have collected several objects, as a group, arrange them to make a human figure or face.

3. Share your sculpture with the class and discuss how unity occurs in each form. How is variety used? How is harmony used?

◀ **Alan McCormack.**
Age 12.

Think about how the student artist used unity in this sculpture.

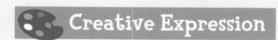

Creative Expression

How can you use unity to create a human or animal form using discarded machine or technology parts?

1. Begin by collecting a variety of machine and/or technology parts. Look at your list in your Art Journal for ideas. Place any extra objects you have in an area to share with your classmates.

2. Place your collected objects on your table and try to create a human or animal form. Arrange your items until you find an arrangement you like.

3. Create a class display with your completed sculpture and those of your classmates.

Art Criticism

Describe List the objects you used in your sculpture. Describe the form you made. Is it an animal or a person?

Analyze Describe how you used variety and harmony to create unity in your sculpture.

Interpret Give your sculpture a title. Create a fantasy story based on your sculpture.

Decide Were you successful in using unity in your sculpture? Explain.

Variety, Harmony, and Unity

▲ **Benny Andrews.** (American).
Grandmother's Dinner. 1992.

Oil on canvas. 72 × 52 inches (182.88 × 132.08 cm.).
Ogden Museum of Southern Art, New Orleans, Louisiana.

Art Criticism | Critical Thinking

Describe **What do you see?**

During this step you will collect information about the subject of the work.

▶ Describe the people, including their clothing and their postures.

▶ Describe the environment and the objects in it.

Analyze **How is this work organized?**

Think about how the artist used the elements and principles of art.

▶ How did the artist use contrast of colors to create variety?

▶ How did he use contrast of lines to create variety?

▶ How did he use shapes to create harmony?

▶ How did he make this work a unified composition?

Interpret **What does the artwork say?**

Combine clues you collected during description and analysis with your personal experiences to find out what this painting is about.

▶ What do you think is the story behind this painting?

▶ What is the location of this room?

▶ Why do you think there is a high-intensity blue on the boy's jeans when all the other colors are tints?

Decide **What do you think about the work?**

Use all the information you have gathered to decide why this is a successful work of art.

▶ Is this successful because it is realistic, because it is well organized, and/or because it conveys a message?

Show What You Know

Answer these questions on a separate sheet of paper.

1 An _____ is a variety of objects put together to create one complete piece.
A. abstract
B. application
C. assemblage

2 _____ is the principle of art that relates to differences or contrasts.
A. Variety
B. Unity
C. Harmony

3 _____ is the feeling of wholeness or oneness that is achieved by properly using the elements and principles of art.
A. Unity
B. Harmony
C. Variety

4 _____ is the principle of art that creates unity by stressing similarities of separate but related parts.
A. Variety
B. Harmony
C. Unity

5 When an artist creates unity, he or she harmonizes _____, or the different elements or objects, by making them relate to one another.
A. symmetry
B. variety
C. emphasis

VISIT A MUSEUM
Dallas Museum of Art

The Dallas Museum of Art began as the Dallas Art Association. It was founded in 1903, and its name was changed to the Dallas Museum of Art in 1984. The museum's permanent collection includes Asian, African, Indonesian, and contemporary art, as well as photography, pre-Columbian, impressionist and post-impressionist European art. The sculpture collection is displayed both indoors and outdoors. The museum also has a model of a French country house that contains works by Renoir, van Gogh, Gauguin, Cézanne, and Degas.

Variety, Harmony, and Unity in Animation

John Ramirez is an animator and storyboard artist for feature animated films. His video "Every Picture Tells a Story" shows how he works with a creative team to make an animated film. He studies photographs of real people and scenes to know how to draw them in his storyboards.

What to Do Create a short story that is expressed in a four-frame comic strip.

Comic strips are a simple form of storyboarding. They have four frames in which to tell a joke or simple story. The style of art and the characters' postures and expressions are also integral to the success of the idea. They show the movement, pattern, and sequence of an idea from the beginning to the end.

1. Think of a simple idea or joke. Your idea should have specific characters and a beginning, middle, or end.

2. Sketch out four scenes to show the action in the story. You can also add simple dialogue or captions.

3. Use contrast to keep the viewer's attention on a specific part of your drawing. Give your characters a name, add dialogue, and title your strip.

4. Share your strip with your friends. Ask them if they understand the story.

▲ John Ramirez. "Every Picture Tells a Story."

Art Criticism

Describe Describe the scenes you chose to convey your idea or story.

Analyze How did you choose the four scenes that would best tell your story?

Interpret How did you use contrast to emphasize the point of your joke or story?

Decide Did you use some elements (line, shape, color, etc.) to create variety, and some elements to create unity?

Technique Tips
Embroidery

Running stitch

The running stitch is the simplest and most basic of all stitches. Pass the needle in and out of the fabric, making the surface stitches equal in length. The stitches on the underside should also be of equal length, but half the size or shorter than the upper stitches.

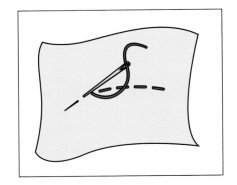

Back stitch

Bring the thread up through on the stitch line and then take a small stitch backward through the fabric. Bring the needle through again a little in front of the first stitch, then take another stitch, inserting the needle at the point where it first came through.

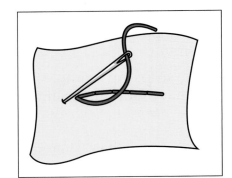

Couching

Working from left to right, position the thread or threads on the fabric. Use your thumb to hold it in place. Bring out the working couching thread from underneath the fabric, just below the laid thread. Secure the laid thread at regular intervals with a couching stitch. Finish at the end of the line by taking both the couching thread and the laid thread to the back of the fabric.

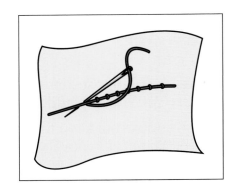

Outline stitch

The outline stitch creates a neat twisted line. Work from left to right along the line of the design, taking small regular stitches with a forward and backward motion. The thread is kept to the left of the needle after picking up a small piece of material.

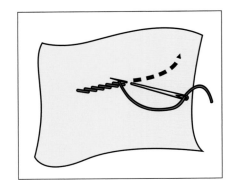

Technique Tips

Drawing

Pencil

With a pencil, you can add form to your objects with shading. With the side of your pencil lead, press and shade over areas more than once for darker values. You can also use lines or dots for shading. When lines or dots are drawn close together, darker values are created. When dots or lines are drawn farther apart, lighter values are created.

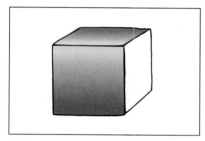

Blending

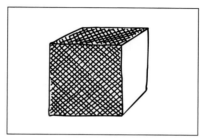

Cross-hatching

Hatching

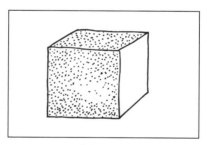

Stippling

Technique Tips

Color Pencil

You can blend colors with color pencils. Color with the lighter color first. Gently color over it with the darker color until you have the effect you want.

With color pencils, you can use the four shading techniques.

Shadows can be created by blending complementary colors.

Technique Tips

Fine-Point Felt-Tip Pen

Fine-point felt-tip pens can be used to make either sketches or finished drawings. They are ideal for contour drawings.

Use the point of a fine-point felt-tip pen to make details. Fine-point felt-tip pens can be used for hatching, cross-hatching, and stippling.

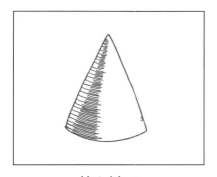

Hatching

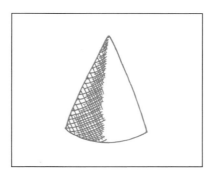

Cross-hatching

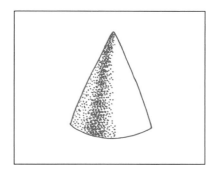

Stippling

Always replace the cap so the fine-point felt-tip pen does not dry out.

Technique Tips

Marker

Markers can be used to make sketches or finished drawings. Use the point of the marker to make thin lines and small dots.

Use the side of the tip for coloring in areas and for making thick lines.

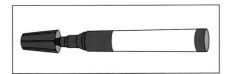

Always replace the cap so the marker does not dry out.

Technique Tips

Color Chalk

Color chalks can be used to make colorful, soft designs.

You can use the tip of the colored chalk to create lines and shapes. You can use the side of the chalk to fill spaces. As with pencil, you can also use them for blending to create shadows.

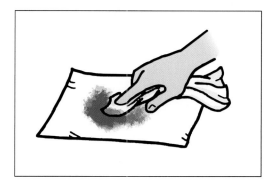

Colored chalk is soft and can break easily. Broken pieces are still usable. Colors can be mixed or blended by smearing them together with your finger or a tissue.

Oil Pastels

Oil pastels are colors that are mixed with oil and pressed into sticks. When you press down hard with them, your pictures will look painted.

Oil pastels are soft with strong colors. You can use oil pastels to color over other media, such as tempera or crayon. Then you can scratch through this covering to create a design.

Technique Tips

Painting

Tempera

1. Fill water containers halfway. Dip your brush in the water. Wipe your brush on the inside edge of the container. Then blot it on a paper towel to get rid of extra water. Stir the paints. Add a little water if a color is too thick or dry. Remember to clean your brush before using a new color.

2. Always mix colors on the palette. Put some of each color that you want to mix on the palette. Then add the darker color a little at a time to the lighter color. Change your water when it gets too cloudy.

3. To create lighter values, add white. To darken a value, add a tiny amount of black. If you have painted something too thickly, add water and blot it with a clean paper towel.

4. Use a thin pointed brush to paint thin lines and details. For thick lines or large areas, press firmly on the tip or use a wide brush.

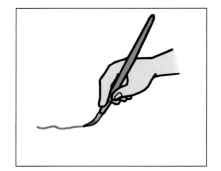 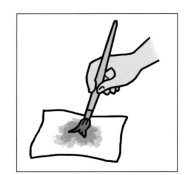

5. Wash your brush when you are finished. Reshape the bristles. Store brushes with bristles up.

Technique Tips

Watercolor

1. Fill water containers halfway. Dip your brush in the water. Wipe your brush on the inside edge of the container. Then blot it on a paper towel to get rid of extra water. With your brush, add a drop of water to each watercolor cake and stir. Remember to clean your brush whenever you change colors.

2. Always mix colors on a palette. Put some of each color that you want to mix on the palette. Then add the darker color a little at a time to the lighter color. Change your water when it gets too dark.

3. To create lighter values, add more water. To darken a value, add a tiny amount of black. If you have painted something too quickly, add water to the paint on the paper and blot it with a clean paper towel.

4. Use a thin pointed brush to paint thin lines and details. For thick lines or large areas, press firmly on the tip or use a wide brush.

5. For a softer look, tape your paper to the table with masking tape. Use a wide brush to add water to the paper, working in rows from top to bottom. This is a wash. Let the water soak in a little. Painting on wet paper will create a soft or fuzzy look. For sharper forms or edges, paint on dry paper, using only a little water on your brush.

6. Wash your brushes when you are finished. Reshape the bristles. Store brushes with the bristles up.

Technique Tips

Acrylic Paint

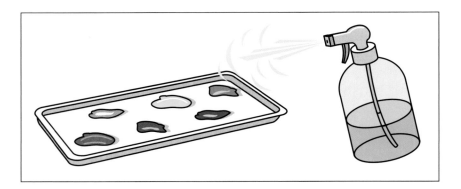

1. Because acrylics dry so fast, squeeze out only a little paint. If you are using a plastic palette, regularly use a spray bottle to spray a fine mist over the paint to keep it moist.

2. Keep a piece of paper towel or cloth next to your water jar, and wipe your brushes on it after you rinse them. When you are not working with your brush, keep it in the water jar.

3. If applied thickly or if mixed with a little white, all acrylic colors can be opaque. If they are diluted, they can be used like watercolors or for airbrushing.

4. Unlike a watercolor wash, when an acrylic wash dries, it is permanent and is insoluble. It can be over-painted without disturbing the existing wash.

5. Because acrylics dry rapidly, you need to work fast to blend colors. If you are working on paper, dampening the paper will increase your working time.

6. Masking tape can be put onto and removed from dried acrylic paint without damaging an existing layer. This makes it easy to produce a sharp edge. Be sure the edges of the tape are firmly pressed down. Do not paint too thickly on the edges, or you will not get a clean line when you lift the tape.

7. When you are finished painting, clean your brushes. Be sure to clean inside the bristles so no paint remains.

Technique Tips

Collograph Print

1. Place your printing plate on a prepared surface. Squeeze some ink onto a tray and smooth it out in a small section to cover your brayer with ink.

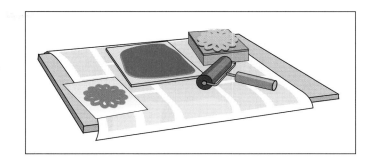

2. Use the brayer to cover the plate with ink. Roll the ink in two directions: up and down and side to side.

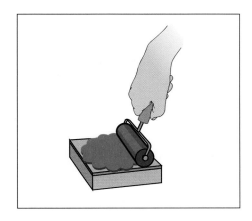

3. Move the plate to a clean area of the table. Place paper on topof the plate and gently rub the top of the paper with your fingers.

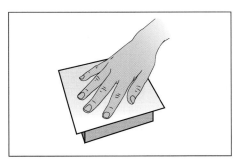

4. Carefully hold the corners of one edge of the paper and lift it off the print. Place the finished print in a safe place to dry.

Technique Tips

Handcoloring a Photograph

If you like, you can make a black and white photograph more interesting by adding color.

1. You can use water-based markers to add color to a photograph.

2. Color pencils create soft colors. Creating layers of color pencil gives a deeper hue.

3. Use a cotton swab to blend in your color pencils and an eraser to remove unwanted marks.

4. Experiment with crayons, oil pastels, and pastel chalks.

Technique Tips

Mobile

There are many ways to put together a mobile, but the assembly is always the same. Start connecting the pieces from the bottom.

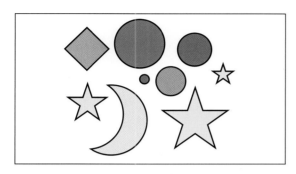

1. Find or create the shapes you want to use. Lay them on a large sheet of paper. Draw lines connecting the bottom, or end, pieces.

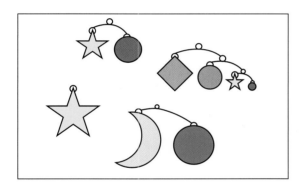

2. Wire the pieces together, starting with the small end pieces. Then connect the middle-size systems together.

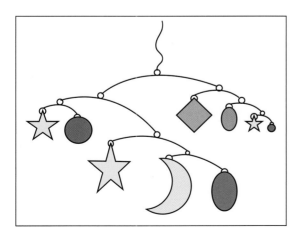

3. Connect the top bar last. Connect the middle systems to the top bar, then balance and hang the mobile.

Technique Tips

Collage

In a collage, objects or pieces of paper, fabric, or other materials are pasted onto a surface to create a work of art. When planning your collage, consider such things as:

- Size of shapes and spaces
- Placement of shapes and spaces
- Color schemes
- Textures

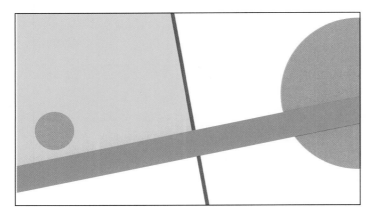

Remember that the empty (negative) spaces are also part of your design. Plan a collage as you would plan a painting or a drawing. After deciding what shapes and objects you want to use, arrange them on the paper. When you have made an arrangement you like, glue your shapes and objects to the paper.

Technique Tips
Weaving

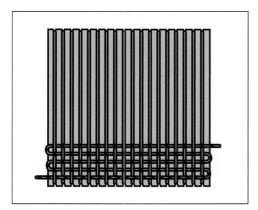

1. Measure and cut notches one-quarter inch apart and one-half inch deep on opposite sides of the cardboard.

2. Tape the warp thread to the back and string from top to bottom. Continue to wrap the thread through each notch until you reach the end. Tape the end of the thread to the cardboard.

3. Start to weave horizontally at the bottom of the loom in an over-one-under-one motion.

4. Do not pull the weft threads too tight.

Technique Tips

Sculpting

Clay

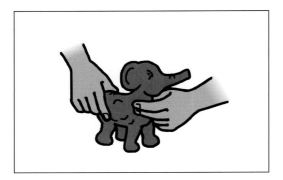

Pinch and pull clay into the desired shape.

Joining Two Pieces of Clay

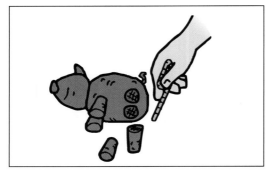

Score, or scratch, both pieces so they will stick together.

Attach the pieces with some *slip,* which is watery clay.

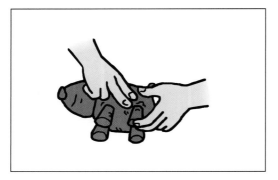

Squeeze the two pieces together.
Smooth the edges.

Technique Tips

Clay Slab Construction

To roll a slab of clay, press a ball of clay into a flat shape on a cloth-covered board. Place one $\frac{1}{4}$-inch slat on each side of the clay. Use a roller to press the slab into an even thickness. With a straightened paper clip, trim the slab into the desired shape.

Wrap unfinished sculptures in plastic to keep them moist until finished.

When you are constructing a form such as a container or house with slabs of clay, it may be necessary to stuff the form with wads of newspaper to support the walls. The newspaper will burn out in the kiln.

Activity Tips

Line and Qualities of Line

🎨 Creative Expression

1. Look over the directions you wrote in your Art Journal on how to make a contour drawing. Make a practice drawing of your object, or objects, following your directions.

2. Using a marker, make a second drawing of the same object.

3. Make some lines thick and some lines thin. You may pick up your marker and look at your paper to make the thick and thin lines. Always concentrate on the contours of your object.

4. Look at your first contour drawing and compare it to your second one.

Geometric and Free-Form Shapes

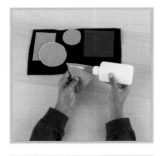

🎨 Creative Expression

1. Collect your pattern pieces from the Practice activity. Select a background square in the color that best depicts the time or place of your scene. Select various colors of felt for each of your pattern pieces.

2. Use a piece of chalk or a pencil to outline the paper shapes onto the felt pieces. Cut out the felt shapes and arrange them on the background square. Secure your shapes with either straight pins or a dot of craft glue.

3. Thread your needle and stitch the cut shapes into place on the background. Look at the embroidery Technique Tips on page 214 to get ideas for different stitches to use.

Activity Tips

Geometric Forms

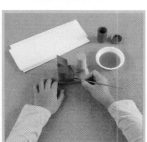

Creative Expression

1. Look at the sketches in your Art Journal and collect the wooden forms you will need.

2. Use either wood glue or craft glue to put your sculpture together. You may need to use a hot-glue gun and sticks for those pieces that will not hold together. Ask your teacher for assistance with this.

3. As you glue your pieces together, see if your sculpture will stand on its own. You may need to make adjustments to your sculpture as you work.

4. Apply acrylic paint to your sculpture once the glue has dried completely. You may want to test colors on a scrap piece of paper before using it on the wood.

Free-Form Form

Creative Expression

1. Look at the sketches you drew in your Art Journal and select one. On sketch paper, make simple contour line drawings of the main forms for your model.

2. Cut a piece of thin wire so that it is about three inches longer than the contour of your drawing. Start at the bottom of the drawing and trace around the object using the wire. Leave about $1\frac{1}{2}$ inches of extra wire at the beginning. As you bend your wire around the line, tape it in place. When you reach the bottom where you started, twist the two ends together so that you form a stake, or stick.

3. Cover your wire shapes with tissue paper.

4. Color your base with acrylic paints. Construct your model by pushing the wire stakes or sticks into the base.

Activity Tips

Space and Perspective

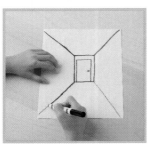

Creative Expression

1. Using a pencil, draw a horizontal or vertical rectangle in the center of your paper, no larger than three inches. This will be the end of the hall. Draw very lightly.

2. Mark a point near the center of your box—the vanishing point. Draw four lines with a ruler coming out from that point toward each corner of your paper. These lines will create the walls of your hallway. Add guide lines for the top and bottom of doors or objects on the walls or in the hall.

3. Outline your drawing with a marker. Erase any unnecessary guide lines. Use watercolor or color pencils to complete your drawing.

Positive and Negative Space

Creative Expression

1. Look over your selected sketch in your Art Journal. Begin cutting the geometric and free-form shapes for your sculpture. Cut slots and tabs in the shapes to construct your assemblage. Add your features separately, such as eyes, ears, nose, and mouth. Try to create a distinct personality with the facial features.

2. Arrange your shapes on your base as you work. Be sure to include negative space within your sculpture. Glue your sculpture to the base.

3. Use acrylic paints and a marker to add color and details. Glue your collected items to your sculpture to embellish it. Give your completed sculpture a descriptive title.

Activity Tips

Hue

🎨 Creative Expression

1. Make a pattern of your selected shape or object and trace it twelve times on white paper. Outline your shapes using a permanent marker.

2. Mix only primary colors to make secondary and intermediate colors. Paint your first three shapes the primary colors. Paint the next three shapes the secondary colors. Paint the last shapes the intermediate colors.

3. Once your shapes are dry, cut them out. Arrange them to show the correct color relationships. Your color wheel does not have to be perfectly round, nor does it have to be a wheel. Glue your shapes onto a black or white background once you have your idea.

Value

🎨 Creative Expression

1. Look over your planned sketch in your Art Journal. Lightly transfer your sketch onto your paper, filling the whole page.

2. Select any one color from the color wheel. From your paint palette, mix tints and shades and try them out on a scrap sheet of paper.

3. Paint your landscapes. Using tints and shades of your selected color, make gradual changes in the value in some areas of your painting. Show a wide range of values from almost-white highlights to dark shadows.

Activity Tips

Intensity

Creative Expression

1. Choose your best sketch from your art Journal. Transfer it onto your paper, touching three edges to fill your page.

2. Select any one complementary color set. On a scrap sheet of paper, practice blending colors and creating textures.

3. Color in your portrait with oil pastels. Overlap and blend colors in some areas of your work; use bright colors in other areas. Show both high- and low-intensity colors. Keep your background simple so that it does not distract from the portrait.

- -

Color Schemes

Creative Expression

1. Divide your paper into four equal sections. Fold the paper in half, open it, and fold it in half in the opposite direction.

2. Using your sketch, make a simple line drawing on a small piece of paper. Transfer your line drawing onto each of the rectangles on your drawing paper.

3. Look at the color schemes in this unit, and select any four. Paint each of your four small landscapes using a different color scheme.

4. Use the primary and secondary colors to mix your intermediate colors. Using a small brush, paint the shapes by outlining them with a color. Then use a medium-sized brush to fill them in.

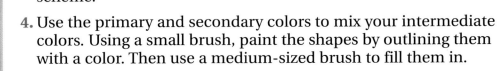

Activity Tips

Visual Texture

🎨 Creative Expression

1. Look over your sketch and draw your image using a computer program. Use any tools or options available on your software to resize and manipulate the image. When your image is completed to your satisfaction, save it as "Original Image."

2. Copy your image and save it as "Drawing 1." Use the fill bucket and other tools to add and create textures.

3. Copy several images and explore a variety of textures from each one. Label and save each drawing as you complete it.

4. Select your three best images to print.

Tactile Texture

🎨 Creative Expression

1. Look over your ideas in your Art Journal. Bring in an old hat to decorate, or make a headpiece from decorated paper. Place collected textured items in a central location to be shared. Keep your personal objects in a separate envelope or bag.

2. Begin by decorating your hat with various real textures, such as beads, ribbon, lace, and fabric. Overlap some of the material, and use thread, yarn, and glue to attach it to your hat base.

3. Next think about how your personal objects will be arranged to convey the theme of your chosen event or memory. Use thread, yarn, and glue to attach your items to your hat.

Activity Tips

Motif and Pattern

🎨 Creative Expression

1. Begin by lightly drawing two or more figures dressed in costume. Refer to your sketches and the student's art above.

2. Look at the motifs you created in the Practice activity. Select one of these to begin a pattern in part of one of the costumes or create a new one. Use a ruler to help you draw straight lines.

3. Continue creating patterns based on your motifs. You may use the same motif again, but change the color.

4. Once your drawing is complete, outline it using a fine-line black marker. Use either color pencils or markers to finish your work.

• •

Two-Dimensional Pattern

🎨 Creative Expression

1. Begin by lightly drawing one large shape off center on your paper. Divide the rest of your paper using straight and curved lines. Have your lines go through your shape. You will have created a variety of shapes.

2. Look at the patterns you created in the Practice activity. Select one of these to begin a pattern in one of the shapes in your design or create a new one. Use a ruler to help you draw straight lines.

3. Continue creating patterns in each shape. Use random, regular, and alternating patterns.

4. Use either color pencils or markers to finish your patterns and complete your work.

Activity Tips

Three-Dimensional Pattern

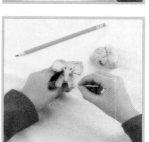

🎨 Creative Expression

1. Begin by forming your clay animal.

2. Once you have your basic animal form, add ears. You can either pinch out or attach the ear forms.

3. Think about other details that are important for your particular animal, like eyes and feet. When you have finished forming your animal, use a toothpick or pencil to add details.

4. Paint your animal using one or two base colors. Once the base color has dried, add patterns using a thin brush or paint pen. Dots and lines can be layered on top of one another.

Rhythm

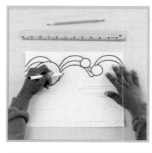

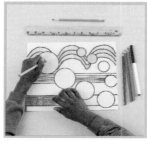

🎨 Creative Expression

1. Select a shape and a line. Repeat parallel lines and shapes to create visual rhythm. Place them so that your entire paper is covered. Make your design nonobjective; there should be no recognizable objects in your composition.

2. Once your design is drawn to your satisfaction, use a felt-tip marker to trace over your lines.

3. Look at the color schemes in Unit 2. Select one color scheme to use in your nonobjective design. Use color pencils to add color to complete your design.

Activity Tips

Visual Movement

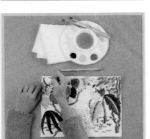

🎨 Creative Expression

1. Look over your sketches and select several of your images to transfer onto your drawing paper. Choose at least one animal to include in your composition and lightly draw it in first. As you draw, fill in any open spaces with overlapping plant shapes.

2. Practice mixing a variety of greens and testing them on a scrap piece of paper. Do this with any color you mix before applying it to your painting.

3. Begin painting the objects in your drawing. First outline your shape with a small paintbrush, then fill it in.

4. Create an area of interest by using a lighter color or a different shape.

Kinetic Movement

🎨 Creative Expression

1. Look over your list in the Ideas section of your Art Journal. Select one subject and begin by sketching simple shapes or objects.

2. Select five or seven of your images to transfer onto your pieces of mat board. Punch a hole in the top of each shape. Use sandpaper to smooth out the cut edges of your board by sanding in one direction.

3. Use acrylic paints to paint your shapes.

4. Lay out your shapes on a large piece of newspaper. Draw the wire lines showing how the pieces will connect. Begin at the bottom and work your way up.

5. Follow the Mobile Technique Tip and connect your mobile. Attach the top bar last.

Activity Tips

Formal Balance and Symmetry

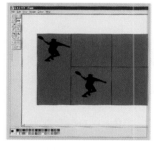

🎨 Creative Expression

1. Use one of the ideas in your Art Journal to create two sketches. Use basic shapes and architectural elements. Look at the architectural details that you collected in your Art Journal for ideas.

2. Look over your two sketches and decide which one you like best. Lightly transfer your sketch onto drawing paper. Use a ruler to help you draw straight lines.

3. Add architectural textures such as wood or stone to make your design more interesting. Decide where your building will be located and add a background.

4. After your drawing is complete, outline it using a fine-tipped black marker. Use watercolor paints to complete your design.

Approximate Symmetry

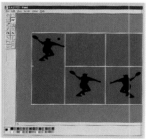

🎨 Creative Expression

1. Look at your collected images in your art Journal. Choose one or two images.

2. Use a computer draw or paint program and the mouse to draw your interpretation of the selected images. Do not include anything from the images' background.

3. Create a copy of your images and save them. Use a variety of tools on the menu to create a design using approximate symmetry.

4. After your drawing is complete, select either a warm or cool color for your background. Create interest by using a contrasting color to complete your design. Title and save your work.

Activity Tips

Informal Balance

🎨 Creative Expression

1. Arrange a variety of objects to create a still life. Include tall and short objects and items with various patterns and colors.

2. Create two quick sketches from different viewpoints using asymmetrical balance. Select the one you like best.

3. Use white chalk to transfer your sketch onto black paper. Use white glue to outline your drawing. Let it dry.

4. Use color chalk to add color to your still-life drawing.

5. Give your completed work a title.

Radial Balance

🎨 Creative Expression

1. Lightly trace a circle on your paper with eight pie shapes.

2. Draw one shape in the center of your radial design for your focal point. Complete your design by using the shapes you made in your Art Journal. Outline your drawing using a fine-tip permanent marker.

3. Select a color scheme using three or more colors that you like. Use color pencils or markers to complete your radial design.

4. Display it for your classmates to see.

Activity Tips

Emphasis of an Element

Creative Expression

1. You will be layering each of your shapes to create a collage of your image. Look at your plant sketch in your Art Journal. Draw and cut out your large shape first. If you are creating a flower, cut out the individual petals and glue these on top of your paper. Glue the center portion last. This is called a printing plate.

2. Once you have glued down all of your shapes, make a crayon rubbing of it. This will allow you to see what your print will look like when it is finished. Make any necessary changes.

3. Set up your printing area and create a print of your collaged image.

Emphasis of Area

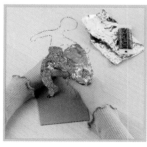

Creative Expression

1. Review your list of locations in your art Journal. As a class, select one location. Look over your Practice gesture drawings and select one or create a new one.

2. Create a wire figure based on your selected gesture. The wire figure is an armature, the framework for supporting the foil that will be used for your sculpture.

3. Using pieces of aluminum foil no larger that your hand, cover the wire sculpture. You can pinch out a nose or add clothing with more foil.

4. Attach your completed foil sculpture to a base, if necessary. As a class, arrange your sculptures for display.

Activity Tips

Facial Proportions

Creative Expression

1. Choose one of the sketches from your Art Journal. Begin by using chalk to draw in your facial proportions. Add your features, hair, and clothing to fill the page.

2. Select a color scheme that you think best reflects your personality.

3. Practice blending colors on a scrap piece of paper. Do this by overlapping colors and working them with your oil pastels. Try using a paper towel to blend colors.

4. Use oil pastels to complete your self-portrait.

Figure Proportions

Creative Expression

1. Take turns with your partner posing for one another and making several sketches. Use the sighting technique. Think about body proportions as you create your sketches.

2. Select the sketch you like best and transfer it to drawing paper. Add a prop to your drawing that looks like it belongs, such as a tennis racket. Use a combination of simple thick and thin lines, and draw your image large so that your figure fills the page. Include a background in your drawing.

3. Use a marker to outline your drawing and to add textures. Use hatching, cross-hatching, or stippling techniques to create value.

Activity Tips

Facial Distortion

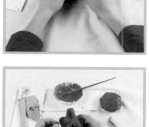

🎨 Creative Expression

1. Create various sketches of a face jug and select one. Look at your selected sketch, and then make a clay sphere. Gently pat your form, turning it in your hands to make it even all around. Flatten the bottom to sit upright.

2. Pinch out a spout at the top of your form, but do not make a hole. Lightly draw the facial features.

3. Form and attach the features using the scoring method. Make the eyes from small balls of clay, and make the lids from small coils of clay.

4. Use a pencil to pierce a hole in the spout as you support it with your fingers. Add color with glaze.

Figure Distortion

🎨 Creative Expression

1. Use a digital camera, and take several photographs of a family member or friend. Choose one or two of your photographs.

2. Begin by loading the image into the computer. If you have regular photographs, scan them into the computer.

3. Use a draw or paint program to create a copy of the image, and then save it. Use a variety of tools on the menu to create a distortion of the image.

4. Add textures to the background or alter the colors. Title and save your work.

Activity Tips

Realistic Scale

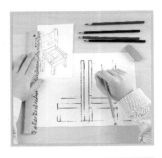

Creative Expression

1. Look at the list of rooms and images in your Art Journal. Select one of the people from the Practice activity as your client.

2. Begin planning a chair for your client. Think about where it will be used and the image you will use for your design. Create several sketches until you make one you like.

3. Use a pencil and a ruler to draw your chair to scale.

4. Use color pencils to add details and to complete your design.

Unrealistic Scale

Creative Expression

1. Begin by sketching several designs. Select your best one. Look at the collected cutouts in your Art Journal and place them on the table. Select three of the images to use in your collage.

2. Look through magazines to find at least four examples of natural elements, such as trees and rocks. Cut these out.

3. Lightly transfer your sketch onto paper. Combine your collected images to create a surreal collage.

4. Use oil pastels to add color and complete your work.

Activity Tips

Variety through Line, Shape, and Color

🎨 Creative Expression

1. Select your best sketch from your Art Journal or create a new one. Then select a colored sheet of paper for your background.

2. Begin by cutting out the shape of the person or animal from paper whose color contrasts with your background color.

3. Use a variety of colors and shapes to cut out objects for your environment. Overlap your shapes to make them more interesting.

4. Glue your arrangement in place. Use a felt-tip marker to make a variety of repeated lines to complete your collage.

Variety Through Contrast

🎨 Creative Expression

1. Decide on a theme and take several black-and-white photographs.

2. Look at your developed images carefully. Choose one or two photographs that show a range of gray values. Put these aside to hand-color.

3. Select a third image for practice. Review the Hand-Coloring a Photograph Technique Tips. Experiment with the various techniques.

4. Add variety to your two selected images by adding color to one area in each photograph. Use one hand-coloring technique you like for each image.

Activity Tips

Harmony in Two-Dimensional Art

Creative Expression

1. Look over your planned sketch in your Art Journal or create a new one. Use a light piece of chalk to transfer your design to the burlap. Make your image large, and keep your design simple.

2. Use masking tape to tape around the edges of the burlap before you begin stitching. This will keep it from unraveling.

3. Look at your practice embroidery piece and the Technique Tips on page 214. Outline your image first using either a running, back, or outline stitch. Use a contrasting color of yarn and a satin stitch to complete your work. Make sure you have used at least one art element in your embroidery to create harmony.

Harmony in Three-Dimensional Art

Creative Expression

1. Look over the list of recycled objects in your Art Journal and try to collect several of the objects.

2. Begin by arranging the objects in the box. None of the objects should stick out beyond one inch from the box's edge. Think about repeating similar shapes in one area of the box and using different shapes in another area.

3. Once you have arranged your objects, glue them in place. Use one harmonious color to paint all of the assemblages of your group members. Arrange the individual works to create one or two harmonious sculptures.

Activity Tips

Unity in Weaving

 **Creative Expression**

1. Prepare your loom following the Weaving Technique Tips. Look at your loom design in your Art Journal. Select your yarn and attach it to your first warp string.

2. Begin by using the tabby (basket) weave for the first few rows to get used to the rhythm of weaving.

3. Look at your sketch and try to follow your plan. You may find as you work that you need to make adjustments to your design.

4. When you are finished, take your weaving off the loom.

Unit 6 · Lesson 6 **Unity in Three-Dimensional Art**

Creative Expression

1. Begin by collecting a variety of machine and/or technology parts. Look at your list in your Art Journal for ideas. Place any extra objects you have in an area to share with your classmates.

2. Place your collected objects on your table and try to create a human or animal form. Arrange your items until you find an arrangement you like.

3. Create a class display with your completed sculpture and those of your classmates.

Visual Index

Artist Unknown
Dancing Lady
c. 50 B.C. (page 161)

Leonardo da Vinci
Ginevra de' Benci
c. 1474. (page 180)

Royal Workshops
Armor of George Clifford,
Third Earl of Cumberland
1580–1585. (page 160)

Rembrandt van Rijn
Portrait of Rembrandt
1650. (page 124)

Thornton, Latrobe, Bulfinch,
and Walter
United States Capitol
18th–19th centuries.
(page 126)

Giovanni Paolo Pannini
The Picture Gallery of
Cardinal Silvio Valenti
Gonzaga
1749. (page 52)

John Singleton Copley
Henry Pelham (Boy with
a Squirrel)
1765. (page 157)

Jean-Baptiste Simeon Chardin
Still Life with the Attributes of
the Arts
1766. (page 83)

Artist Unknown
Ceremonial Skirt
19th century. (page 37)

Katsushika Hokusai
Li Bai (Imagery of the Poets)
1834. (page 134)

William Sharp
Great Water Lily of America
1854. (page 143)

Mary Cassatt
The Tea
1879. (page 135)

Paul Cézanne
Bottom of the Ravine
1879. (page 113)

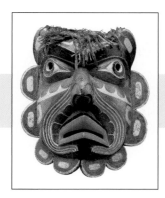

Artist Unknown
Face Mask of K̓umugwe'
c. 1880. (page 96)

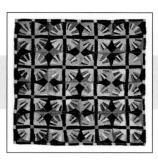

Artist Unknown
Quilt
c. 1885. (page 40)

Alexandre-Gustave Eiffel
Eiffel Tower
1887–1889. (page 127)

James Ensor
Fireworks
1887. (page 78)

Vincent van Gogh
Café Terrace at Night
1888. (page 53)

Vincent van Gogh
Portrait of Joseph Roulin
1888. (page 70)

John Henry Twachtman
Snow Scene
1882. (page 71)

Mary Cassatt
Mother and Child
c. 1890. (page 90)

Paul Gauguin
The Brooding Woman
(Te Faaturuma)
1891. (page 184)

Edvard Munch
The Scream
1893. (page 164)

Harriet Powers
Pictorial Quilt
1895–1898. (page 41)

Auguste Renoir
Young Spanish Woman
with a Guitar
1898. (page 64)

Artist Unknown
Akrafokonmu (Soul Discs)
20th century. (page 139)

Artist Unknown
Coming of Age Hat
20th century. (page 87)

Artist Unknown
Egungun from Ogbomoso
20th century. (page 97)

Artist Unknown
Face Jugs
20th century. (page 165)

Artist Unknown
Carved Animals
20th century. (page 105)

Paul A. Baliker
Fish Story
20th century. (page 48)

Nathaniel Bustion
Bo Bo Festival Series #3
20th century. (page 186)

Susan Le Van
Two Birds in Hand
20th century. (page 82)

Julia Russell
Leonardo da Vinci Chair
20th century. (page 173)

John Warren
Dark Snapper
20th century. (page 49)

Alverda Herb (attributed to)
Bull's Eye Quilt
1900–1920. (page 138)

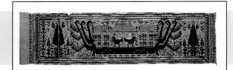

Artist Unknown
Ceremonial Hanging
c. 1900. (page 203)

Gustav Klimt
Die Erfüllung (Fulfillment)
1905–1909. (page 34)

Ferdinand Hodler
James Vibert, Sculptor
1907. (page 131)

Georges Braque
Fishing Boats
1909 and 1911.
(page 79)

Henri Rousseau
Exotic Landscape
1910. (page 112)

George Bellows
Cliff Dwellers
1913. (page 60)

André Derain
*Portrait of a Young Girl
in Black*
1914. (page 74)

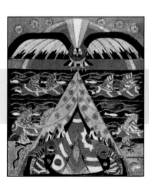

Marsden Hartley
Indian Fantasy
1914. (page 100)

Franz Marc
Animals in a Landscape
1914. (page 108)

Stanton MacDonald Wright
Conception Synchromy
1914. (page 67)

Max Weber
Chinese Restaurant
1915. (page 94)

**Louisa Keyser
(Dat So La Lee)**
Basket
c. 1917–1918.
(page 202)

Karl Schmidt-Rottluff
Portrait of Emy
1919. (page 75)

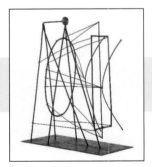

Pablo Picasso
*Proposal for a Monument
to Apollinaire*
1928. (page 57)

Artist Unknown
King's Crown
c. 1930. (page 86)

Salvador Dalí
Persistence of Memory
1931. (page 176)

Frida Kahlo
Frida y Diego Rivera
1931. (page 154)

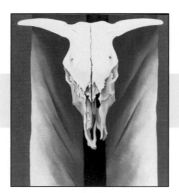

Georgia O'Keeffe
Cow's Skull: Red White and Blue
1931. (page 130)

Henri Matisse
Plate 24 from Poésies by Stéphane Mallarmé
1932. (page 36)

Artist Unknown
Woman's Headcloth
c. 1935–1945. (page 195)

Isabel Bishop
Two Girls
1935. (page 156)

Pablo Picasso
Portrait of Dora Maar
1938. (page 109)

Alexander Calder
Lobster Trap and Fish Tail
1939. (page 116)

Grandma Moses
Mt. Nebo on the Hill
c. 1940. (page 194)

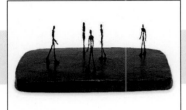

Alberto Giacometti
City Square
1948. (page 168)

Minnie Evans
King
1962. (page 101)

David Smith
Cubi XVII
1963. (page 44)

Pablo Picasso
Chicago Picasso
1967. (page 177)

Moshe Safdie
Habitat
1967. (page 172)

Alice Neel
Loneliness
1970. (page 150)

Loiuse Nevelson
White Vertical Water
1972. (page 198)

Susan Rothenberg
Cabin Fever
1976. (page 142)

Teodora Blanco
Ceramic Figures
1978. (page 104)

George Segal
Three People on Four Park Benches
1979. (page 147)

Fernando Botero
Dancing in Colombia
1980. (page 169)

Wayne Thiebaud
Down Eighteenth Street
1980. (page 120)

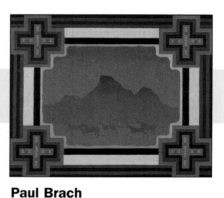

Paul Brach
Chuska
1982. (page 191)

Miriam Schapiro
Anna and David
1987. (page 66)

Benny Andrews
Grandmother's Dinner
1992. (page 210)

Lee Bennion
Snow Queen, Portrait of Adah
1992. (page 187)

Juan Muñoz
Last Conversation Piece
1994–1995. (page 146)

David Bates
Seated Man #4
1995. (page 56)

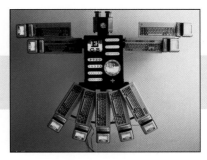

Nam June Paik
Eagle Eye
1996. (page 206)

Randy Ellett
National Parts
1996. (page 199)

George Hart
Roads Untaken
1998. (page 45)

Timothy Rose
Double Pan Swoosh
2001. (page 117)

Christina Lemon
Mask Brooch
2003. (page 207)

Roz Ragans
Pas de Deux
2003. (page 190)

Glossary

A

alternating pattern
(ôl' tər nāt ing pat' ərn), *noun* Can repeat a motif, but change position; alter spacing between motifs or add a second motif

analogous colors (ə nal' ə gəs kul' ərs), *noun* Colors that sit side by side on the color wheel and have a common hue. Violet, blue-violet, blue, blue-green are examples of analogous colors.

appliqué (ap' li kā), *noun* Decoration made from cloth cutouts and applied, usually through embroidery, onto a background cloth

approximate symmetry (ə 'präk sə mət sim' i trē), *noun* A type of formal balance that is almost symmetrical but small differences in the artwork make it more interesting

armature (är' mə chər), *noun* A framework for supporting material used in sculpting

assemblage (ä säm bläzh'), *noun* A sculpture technique in which a variety of objects is assembled to create one complete piece

asymmetrical balance
(ā sim' i tri cəl bal' əns), *noun* Another name for informal balance

atmospheric perspective
(ət mos fer ik per spek' tiv), *noun* The effects air and light have on how we perceive an object

B

background (bak' ground'), *noun* The area of the picture plane farthest from the viewer

balance (bal' əns), *noun* The principle of design that deals with visual weight in an artwork

blending (blen ding), *noun* A shading technique that creates a gradual change from light to dark or dark to light

body proportion (bod' ē prə pôr shən), *noun* The size relationship of one part of the body to another

C

central axis (sen' trəl ak' sis), *noun* A real or imaginary dividing line which can run in two directions, vertically and horizontally

collage (kō läzh), *noun* A two-dimensional work of art made up of pieces of paper and/or fabric to create the image.

collograph (kə lō graf), *noun* A print-making technique where cut papers or thin boards are arranged to create an image on a stiff printing plate.

color (kul' ər), *noun* 1. The art element that is derived from reflected light; 2. In balance: a brighter color has more visual weight than a dull color; 3. In perspective: bright-colored objects seem closer, while dull or pale objects appear farther away.

color scheme (kul' ər skēm'), *noun*
A plan for organizing the colors used in an artwork

color spectrum (kul' ər spek' trum), *noun* The effect that occurs when light passes through a prism and separates into a band of colors in the order of red, orange, yellow, green, blue, and violet

color wheel (kul' ər 'wēl), *noun* Shows the color spectrum bent into a circle

complementary colors (kom' plə men tə rē kul' ərz), *noun* Colors that are opposite each other on the color wheel

complex geometric shapes (kom' pleks jē' ə met' rik shāps), *noun* Combined basic geometric shapes: a pentagon or hexagon

contour line (kon' tür līn), *noun* Defines the edges and surface ridges of an object

contrast (kon' trast), *noun* 1. A technique for creating a focal point or area of interest in a work of art using differences in elements; 2. In emphasis: contrast occurs when one element stands out from the rest of the work.

converging lines (kən vərg ing līnz), *noun* One of the six perspective techniques. Parallel lines seem to converge or move toward the same point as they move away from you.

cool colors (kül kul' erz), *noun* Green, violet, and blue. They suggest coolness and move away from the viewer.

cross-hatching (krôs hach' ing), *noun* A shading technique created when sets of parallel lines cross or intersect

curved (kûrvd), *adj.* A line that bends and changes gradually or turns inward to form spirals

D

detail (dē tāl), *noun* One of the six perspective techniques. Objects with fuzzy, blurred edges appear farther away than those with clear sharp edges.

diagonal (dī ag' ə nəl), *noun (adj.)* A line that moves on a slant

directional lines (di rekt' shən' al līnz), *noun* How a line moves: diagonally, vertically, or horizontally

distortion (di stôr shən), *noun* A deviation from normal or expected proportions

E

elongate (ē' lôn gāt), *verb* To stretch out or make long

embroidery (im broi də rē), *noun* The art of decorating designs with needle and thread

emphasis (em' fə sis), *noun* The principle of design that stresses one area in an art work over another area

exaggeration (eg zaj' ə rā' shən), *noun* To increase or enlarge beyond what is expected or normal

F

facial proportions (fā' shəl prə pôr shənz), *noun* The relationship of one feature of a face to another feature

focal point (fo' kəl point'), *noun* The point which the receding lines meet. It is the first part of a composition to attract the viewer's attention.

foreground (fôr' ground'), *noun* The area of the picture plane that is closest to the viewer

form (form), *noun* A three-dimensional object that is measured by height, width, and depth

formal balance (fôr' mel bal' əns), *noun* Occurs when equal or similar elements are placed on opposite sides of a central axis

free-form forms (frē' fôrm' fôrmz), *noun* Three-dimensional forms with irregular edges often found in nature

free-form shapes (frē' fôrm' shāps), *noun* Two-dimensional images made of straight or curved lines or a combination of both

freestanding sculpture (frē stan' ding skulp' chər), *noun* A three-dimensional work of art that can be viewed on all sides because it is surrounded by space

frontal proportions (frən' təl prə pôr' shənz), *noun* A front view of the head that is divided by three horizontal lines across the central axis

futurists (fyü' chə' rists), *noun* A group of Italian artists during the early twentieth-century who repeated and overlapped shapes and lines, to create the illusion of movement

G

geometric forms (je' ə met' rik fôrmz), *noun* Mathematically precise forms based on geometric shapes

geometric shapes (je' ə met' rik shāps), *noun* Mathematically precise shapes: circle, square, and triangle

gesture drawings (jes' chər drô' ing), *noun* Quick drawings used to capture the position or pose of the body

H

harmony (här' mə nē), *noun* The principle of art which creates unity by stressing similarities of separate but related parts

hatching (hach' ing), *noun* A shading technique that looks like a series of parallel lines

high-intensity color (hī in ten' si te kul' ər), *noun* A pure hue such as red

horizontal (hôr' ə zon təl), *noun* A line that moves from side to side

hue (hū), *noun* Another name for color

I

informal balance (in fôr'məl bal' əns), *noun* A way of organizing parts of a design so that unlike objects have equal visual weight

installation (in stäl ā shən), *noun* An artwork which was created for a specific place, such as a gallery or outdoor location

intensity (in ten' si te), *noun* The brightness or dullness of a color

intermediate colors (in' tər m' de it kul' ərs), *noun* Yellow-green, red-orange, blue-green; made by combining a primary with either of the secondary colors that are adjacent on the color wheel

isolation (ī' sə lā' shən), *noun* An object is emphasized by its placement apart from other objects.

K

kinetic movement (kin' e tic müv' mənt), *noun* Actual or real movement

kinetic sculpture (kin' e tic skulp' chər) *noun* A three-dimensional form that actually moves in space

L

line (līn), *noun*   The path of a moving point through space

linear perspective (lin ē' ər pər spek' tiv), *noun*   A system used to create the illusion of depth on a flat surface

location (lō cā' shən), *noun*   Artists can emphasize an object by placing it closer to the center of the piece.

low-intensity color (lō in ten' si te kul' ər), *noun*   A dull hue made by mixing a color with its complement

M

maquette (ma' ket), *noun*   A small model for a larger sculpture

middle ground (mid' əl ground'), *noun*   The area of the picture plane that is usually toward the center

mixed-media (mikst mē dē' ə), *noun*   An art object that has been created from an assortment of media or materials

mobile (mō bēl), *noun*   A moving sculpture in which shapes are balanced and arranged on wire arms and suspended from the ceiling to move freely in the air currents

monochromatic (mon' ə kro mat' ik), *adj.*   A color scheme that is made up of one hue and the tints and shade of that hue

monumental sculptures (mon ū' men' təl skulp' chərz), *noun*   Sculptures that are larger than human forms

motif (mō tēf), *noun*   A unit that is made up of objects or art elements which can be repeated

movement (müv' mənt), *noun*   The principle of art that leads a viewer's eyes throughout a work of art

N

negative space (neg' ə tiv spas'), *noun*   The empty space that surrounds objects, shapes, and forms

neutral colors (nü trəl kul' ərz), *noun*   Black, white, and gray; give hues a range of values

nonobjective (non' əb jek' tiv), *adj.*   Art that has no recognizable subject matter

O

one-point linear perspective (wun' point lin ē' ər pər spek' tiv), *noun*   A system used to create the illusion of depth on a flat surface where all receding lines meet at one point

overlapping (o' vər lap ing), *noun*   1. One object covers a portion of another object. 2. In perspective: one of the six perspective techniques; the object covering another will appear closer to the viewer, creating a feeling of depth.

P

parallel lines (per ə lel līnz), *noun*   Lines that move in the same direction and always stay the same distance apart

pattern (pat' ərn), *noun*   A repeated surface decoration

perspective techniques (pər spek' tiv tek neks'), *noun*   The six techniques an artist uses to create the illusion of depth in two-dimensional art: overlapping, size, placement, detail, color, converging lines

picture plane (pik' chər plān'), *noun*   The surface of a drawing or painting

placement (plās ment), *noun*   One of the six perspective techniques. Objects placed lower in the picture plane appear to be closer than those placed near eye level. There are three areas on a picture plane: foreground, middle ground, and background.

portrait (por trət), *noun*   A two or three-dimensional artwork created in the image of a person or animal

position (pə zish' ən), *noun*   In balance: a larger, positive shape and a small, negative space can be balanced by a small, positive shape and a large, negative space.

positive space (poz' i tiv spas'), *noun*   Refers to any object, shape, or form in two- and three-dimensional art

primary hues (pri' mer ē hūz), *noun*   Red, yellow, and blue, used to mix the other hues on the color wheel

printing plate (print ing plāt), *noun*   A plate that holds the image that will be used to create a print

prism (pri' zm), *noun*   A wedge-shaped piece of glass that bends light as it passes through

profile (prō fīl), *noun*   A side view of a person or animal

profile proportions (prō fīl prə pôr' shənz), *noun*   A side view of the head that is divided by three horizontal lines

proportion (prə pôr' shən), *noun*   The principle of art that is concerned with the size relationship of one part to another

R

radial balance (rā' dē əl bal' əns), *noun*   A type of balance that occurs when the art elements come out, or radiate, from a central point

random pattern (ran' dəm pat' ərn), *noun*   Occurs when the motif is repeated in no apparent order

realistic scale (rē ə lis' tik skāl), *noun*   When an artist creates a work of art where everything fits together and makes sense in size relation

regular pattern (reg' yə lər pat' ərn), *noun*   Occurs when identical motifs are repeated with an equal amount of space between them

rhythm (rith' əm), *noun*   The principle of design that organizes the elements in a work of art by repeating elements and/or objects

S

scale (skāl), *noun*   Size as measured against a standard reference

score (skōr), *verb*   The repeated scratching of the clay surface at the area that another scored piece will be attached

sculpture model (skulp' chər mo' dəl), *noun*   The study or detailed example of what the sculpture will look like when completed

secondary hues (sek' ən der' ē hūz), *noun*   Orange, green and violet; the result of mixing two primary hues

self-portrait (self por trət), *noun*   A two or three-dimensional artwork that an artist makes of him or herself

shade (shād), *noun*   Any hue blended with black

shape (shāp) *noun*   A two-dimensional area that is measured by height and width

simulated texture (sim' u la' təd teks chər), *noun*   Imitates real textures, see also visual texture

size (sīz), *noun*   1. in perspective: objects that are closer look larger than objects that are farther away; 2. In balance: a large shape or form will appear to be heavier than a small shape, and several small shapes can balance one large shape.

slip (slip), *noun*   A mixture of clay and water that is creamy to the touch and is used to attach two scored pieces of clay together

space (spās), *noun*   The art element that refers to the areas above, below, between, within, and around an object

still life (stil' līf'), *noun*   The arrangement of common inanimate objects from which artists draw or paint

stippling (stip' ling), *noun*   A shading technique using dots to show value

surrealism (sə' rē' əl izəm), *noun*   An art movement that emphasized art in which dreams, fantasy, and the subconscious served as inspiration for artists

symmetry (sim' i trē), *noun*   A type of formal balance in which two halves of a balanced artwork are identical, mirror images of each other

T

tactile texture (tak' təl teks' chər), *noun*   Actual texture, texture that can really be felt

texture (teks' chər), *noun*   1. The art element that refers to the way something feels; 2. In balance: a rough texture has an uneven pattern of highlights and shadows. For this reason, a rough surface attracts the viewer's eyes more easily than a smooth, even surface.

three-dimensional patterns (thrē di men' shə nəl pat' ərnz), *noun*   Patterns that have depth and are formed on the surface of a sculptural form

tint (tint), *noun*   Any hue blended with white

two-dimensional decoration (tü' di men' shən nəl dek ə' rā shən), *noun*   Flat decoration produced on the surface of a work of art

U

unity (ū' ni tē), *noun*   The feeling of wholeness or oneness that is achieved by properly using the elements and principles in art

unrealistic scale (un' rē ə lis' tik skāl), *noun*   When an artist makes size relationships that do not make sense

V

value (val' ū), *noun*   The lightness or darkness of a hue

variety (və ri' ə tē), *noun*   The principle of art which is concerned with difference or contrast

vertical (vür' tə kəl), *noun (adj.)*   A line that moves from top to bottom

visual movement (vizh' ü əl müv' mənt), *noun*   Created by repeating an art element or object in a work of art

visual texture (vizh' ü əl teks' chər), *noun*   Or simulated texture, imitates real texture. It is the illusion of a three-dimensional surface.

W

warm colors (wōrm' kul' ərz), *noun*   Red, yellow, and orange. They suggest warmth and come forward toward the viewer.

Z

zigzag (zig' zag) *noun (adj.)*   A line that is made by joining diagonal lines

Index

Photo Credits

Cover Seattle Art Museum, Gift of John H. Hauberg. Photograph by Paul Macapia; 5 © AKG-Images; 6 National Gallery of Art, Washington, D.C. Ailsa Mellon Bruce Collection, Image © 2003 Board of Trustees, National Gallery of Art, Washington; 7 Purchase. Whitney Museum of American Art, New York. Photograph by Geoffrey Clements; 8 National Gallery of Art, Washington D.C. Widener Collection, Image © 2003 Board of Trustees, National Gallery of Art, Washington; 9 San Francisco Museum of Modern Art. © Banco de Mexico Diego Rivera & Frida Kahlo Museum Trust. Av. Cinco de Mayo No.2, Col. Centro, Del. Cuauhtemoc 06059, Mexico, D.F; 10 Worcester Art Museum. Worcester, Massachusetts, museum purchase; 12 (tl) Museum of Fine Arts, Boston: Bequest of John T. Spaulding 48.549, (tr) Hirshhorn Museum and Sculpture Garden, Smithsonian Institution, Gift of Joseph H. Hirshhorn, 1966, (bl) Dallas Museum of Art, Dallas, Texas, (br) © Philip Hayson/Photo Researchers Inc; 13 (tl) Honolulu Academy of Art. Honolulu, Hawaii. Gift of James A. Michener, 1955 (13,694), (tr) Purchased with funds provided by the Smithsonian Collections Acquisition Program. Photograph by Frank Khoury. National Museum of African Art, Smithsonian Institution, Washington D.C., (bl) Image no.EEPA 1474. Eliot Elisofon Photographic Archives, National Museum of African Art, Smithsonian Institution, Washington, D.C., (br) Royal British Columbia Museum, Victoria, Canada; 15 (tl) The Ogden Museum of Southern Art, University of New Orleans, Gift of the Benny Andrews Foundation, (tr) Amon Carter Museum, Fort Worth, Texas. 1999.33.E; 15 (bl) From the Girard Foundation Collection, in the Museum of International Folk Art, a unit of the Museum of New Mexico, Santa Fe, New Mexico. Photographer: Michel Monteaux, (br) © Carl & Ann Purcell/CORBIS; 16 Helen Birch Bartlett Memorial Collection, 1926.252. Photograph © 2001, The Art Institute of Chicago, All Rights Reserved; 17 © Northwest Museum of Arts & Culture. Photo by David Anderson; 18 Wadsworth Atheneum, Hartford. The Ella Gallup Sumner and Mary Catlin Sumner Collection Fund; 19 (t) Dallas Museum of Art, Dallas, Texas, (b) Smithsonian American Art Museum, Washington, DC/Art Resource, NY. © Elizabeth Catlett/Licensed By VAGA, New York, New York; 20 National Gallery, London/Art Resource, NY. Erich Lessing, photographer; 22 (t, tcl, tcr, br, bcr) © Photodisc/Getty Images, Inc, (bcl, bl) © Digital Vision/Getty Images, Inc; 23 (t) © Corbis, (tcl, tcr, bl, bcl, bc) © Photodisc/Getty Images, Inc, (br) © Index Stock Inc; 24, 26, 28, 30 San Francisco Museum of Modern Art. © Banco de Mexico Diego Rivera & Frida Kahlo Museum Trust. Av. Cinco de Mayo No.2, Col. Centro, Del. Cuauhtemoc 06059, Mexico, D.F; 32-33 (t) © Aaron Haupt; 34 © AKG-Images; 35 © Bildarchiv, Österreichische Nationalbibliothek/Sté Nlle des Editions du Chêne; 36 Digital Image © The Museum of Modern Art/Licensed by Scala/Art Resource, NY. © 2004 Succession H. Matisse, Paris/Artists Rights Society (ARS), New York; 37 Dallas Museum of Art; 38 © Eclipse Studios; 39 Randy Ellett; 40 International Folk Art Foundation Collection. Museum of International Folk Art. Santa Fe, New Mexico. Photo by: Pat Pollard; 41 Museum of Fine Arts, Boston: Bequest of Maxim Karolik 64.619; 42 © Eclipse Studios; 43 Randy Ellett; 44 Dallas Museum of Art, Dallas, Texas. Art © Estate of David Smith/Licensed by VAGA, New York, New York; 45 © George Hart; 46 © Eclipse Studios; 47 Randy Ellett; 48 © Paul Baliker; 49 © John Warren; 50 (tl, tc, tr) Photodisc/Getty Images, Inc, (b) © Eclipse Studios; 51 Randy Ellett; 52 Wadsworth Atheneum, Hartford. The Ella Gallup Sumner and Mary Catlin Sumner Collection Fund; 53 © Rijksmuseum Kroller-Muller, Otterlo, Netherlands/Bridgeman Art Library; 54 © Eclipse Studios; 55 Randy Ellett; 56 Dallas Museum of Art, Dallas, Texas; 57 Photo: B. Hatala. Musee Picasso, Paris, France. © Reunion des Musees Nationaux/Art Resource, NY. © 2001 Estate of Pablo Picasso/Artists Rights Society (ARS), New York; 58 © Eclipse Studios; 59 Randy Ellett; 60 Los Angeles County Museum of Art, Los Angeles County Fund; 62 Jeff Kaufman/Taxi/Getty Images, Inc; 63 David Cooper, Vancouver, CANADA; 64 National Gallery of Art, Washington, D.C. Ailsa Mellon Bruce Collection, Image © 2003 Board of Trustees, National Gallery of Art, Washington; 65 © Bettmann/Corbis; 66 © 1997 Miriam Schapiro; 67 Hirshhorn Museum and Sculpture Garden, Smithsonian Institution, Gift of Joseph H. Hirshhorn, 1966; 68 © Eclipse Studios; 69 Randy Ellett; 70 Courtesy of the J. Paul Getty Museum; 71 © Cincinnati Art Museum. Photo by Tony Walsh, 2002; 72 © Eclipse Studios; 73 Randy Ellett; 74 © Hermitage, St. Petersburg, Russia/Bridgeman Art Library; 75 North Carolina Museum of Art, Raleigh, North Carolina. Bequest of W.R. Valentiner. G.65.10.58. © 2004 Artists Rights Society (ARS), New York/VG Bild-Kunst, Bonn; 76 © Eclipse Studios; 77 Randy Ellett; 78 Albright-Knox Art Gallery, Buffalo, New York, George B. and Jenny R. Mathews Fund, 1970. © 2004 Artists Rights Society (ARS), New York/SABAM, Brussels; 79 Museum of Fine Arts, Houston; Gift of Audrey Jones Beck © 2004 Artists Rights Society (ARS), New York/ADAGP, Paris; 80 © Eclipse Studios; 81 Randy Ellett; 82 Bruck and Moss Gallery; 83 © Erich Lessing/Art Resource, NY; 84 (tl, tr, tcl, tcr) Photodisc/Getty Images, Inc, (b) © Eclipse Studios; 87 St. Louis Museum of Art. Museum Shop Fund; 88 (t, tc) Photodisc/Getty Images, Inc, (cl, cr) Getty Images, Inc, (cr) Getty Images, Inc, (b) Eclipse Studios; 89 Randy Ellett; 90 The Roland P. Murdock Collection, Wichita Art Museum, Wichita, Kansas; 92 © Bettmann/Corbis; 93 Craig Schwartz; 94 Purchase. Whitney Museum of American Art, New York. Photograph by Geoffrey Clements; 96 Seattle Art Museum, Gift of John H. Hauberg. Photograph by Paul Macapia; 97 North Carolina Museum of Art, Purchased with funds provided through a bequest from Lucile E. Moorman; 98 © Eclipse Studios; 99 Ko Yoshida; 100 North Carolina Museum of Art, Purchased with funds from the North Carolina Museum of Art; 101 North Carolina Museum of Art, Gift of Mr. and Mrs. D. H. McCollough and the North Carolina Art Society. Robert F. Phifer Bequest; 102 (t, tc) Photodisc/Getty Images, Inc, (b) © Eclipse Studios, (bc) © Royalty-Free/Corbis; 103 Photo by Ko Yoshida; 104 The Nelson A. Rockefeller Collection. San Antonio Museum of Art; 105 Photo by Frank Fortune; 106 (tl) Photodisc/Getty Images, Inc, (tr, b) © Eclipse Studios; 107 Randy Ellett; 108 Detroit Institute of Arts. The Bridgeman Art Library; 109 Hirshhorn Museum and Sculpture Garden, Smithsonian Institution, Gift of